LEARN YOGA
IN A WEEKEND

LEARN YOGA
IN A WEEKEND

THE SIVANANDA YOGA
VEDANTA CENTRE

Photography by Jane Stockman

DORLING KINDERSLEY
London • New York • Stuttgart

A DORLING KINDERSLEY BOOK

Designer Sam Grimmer
Project Editor Sarah Larter
Editor Katie John
Senior Art Editor Amanda Lunn
Series Editors Jo Weeks, Laura Harper
Deputy Art Director Tina Vaughan
Deputy Editorial Director Jane Laing
Production Controller Helen Creeke

First published in Great Britain in 1993
by Dorling Kindersley Limited,
9 Henrietta Street, London WC2E 8PS

A CIP catalogue record for this book
is available from the British Library

ISBN 0-75130-062-4

Computer page make-up by Cloud 9 Designs, Hampshire
Reproduced by Colourscan, Singapore
Printed and bound by Arnoldo Mondadori, Verona, Italy

CONTENTS

Introduction 6

PREPARING FOR THE WEEKEND 8

THE WEEKEND COURSE 24

Day 1

Day 2

AFTER THE WEEKEND 74

INTRODUCTION

ON BEHALF OF the International Sivananda Yoga **Vedanta** Centres, we offer *Learn Yoga In A Weekend* as an inspirational guide to anyone interested in learning about this ancient discipline and enhancing the quality of their lives. The techniques covered in this book were not invented by the Sivananda Yoga Centres, but are historical methods that have been adapted for modern lifestyles by our teacher Swami Vishnu-devananda. Yoga cannot be learned by simply understanding its theory; for it to work, you must put this theory into practice. Although it is not possible to master all the techniques of yoga in a weekend, you can utilize even this short amount of time to begin learning the **asanas**, and use them as a foundation for further development. We think that the step-by-step instructions set out in this book will get you off to a good start. The most effective way to learn yoga is to do a little at a time, and keep to a regular practice schedule. Please be careful not to go beyond your capacity; do not try to work too quickly or too intensively. Although you may wish to learn at home, initially it may be more beneficial to have lessons or take a course with a group, as the collective energy will sustain and inspire you.

Our best wishes are with you.

Swami Saradananda

SWAMI SARADANANDA

PREPARING FOR THE WEEKEND

Getting ready for your weekend of yoga

A YOGA WEEKEND IS AN ADVENTURE of disciplined self-discovery. The exercises, or **asanas**, will unlock tensed muscles, rejuvenate your heart, and restore flexibility to your joints and ligaments. Set aside a quiet time, when you will not be disturbed, for the sessions. If you are at home, you might even want to take the telephone off the hook or put the answering machine on so that you are not distracted. You may practise yoga at any time of the day, but make sure that you have not eaten for several hours, as it is best to do the exercises on an empty stomach. For this reason, many yoga students prefer to practise first thing in the morning. Try to do the asanas in a relaxed manner; do not move abruptly, or you may pull a muscle. Yoga is not a competitive sport; the

ESSENTIAL EXERCISES
Breathing exercises are an essential part of yoga practice. These techniques, which are known as **pranayama**, will clear your lungs, and will help to recharge your physical and mental energy levels. (See pp.20-21.)

UNDERSTANDING BREATHING
In order to perform the breathing exercises and the **asanas** correctly, you must begin by understanding how your lungs work. This knowledge will enable you to make use of their full capacity. (See pp.18-19.)

purpose is to keep you as fit, flexible, and peaceful as possible. Never practise on a bed or soft mattress. A single blanket folded in half or quarters will cushion your body, yet still give you the firm support of the ground. Always wear loose, comfortable clothing, and remember to remove glasses, contact lenses, and jewellery before you begin. During the yoga session, breathe through your nose rather than your mouth, and try to keep your mind focused on your breath. Do not try to go beyond your body's capability.

*Throughout the book you will notice terms printed in **bold** type; these words are defined in the glossary (see pp.92-93).*

TESTING YOUR STRENGTH

Each body has its good points and limitations. Most of us are strong in some ways and supple in others. Factors such as the time of day also make a difference; your muscles are always stiffer in the morning, as they are hardly used while you are asleep. Before you start this course, test the strength and flexibility of each muscle. (See pp.16-17.)

STRETCH AND CONTRACT

The action of each muscle is determined by its line of pull, which is unique to it. If you know where your major muscle groups are, and in which direction they move, you will be able to exercise them more effectively during your yoga sessions. (See pp.14-15.)

PROPER EQUIPMENT

Warm, comfortable surroundings are vital for yoga sessions. Your clothes need not be specially bought, but they must allow your body to move freely. (See pp.12-13.)

WHAT IS YOGA?

Explaining the origins and principles of yoga

THE WORD **YOGA** MEANS "UNION". Yoga is the practical aspect of a philosophy called **Vedanta**, which is set out in the **Upanishads** and maintains that there is one absolute reality that underlies everything in the universe. Yoga techniques have been practised for over 5,000 years. Among the most important teachings of yoga philosophy are instructions on how to put the body under the control of the mind. The Indian sage, Patanjali, defined yoga as being achieved through methods such as controlling the breath and holding the body in steady poses. These techniques are known as **hatha yoga**.

THE FIVE PRINCIPLES

In order for a car to function properly, it requires five things: a lubricating system, a battery, a cooling system, fuel, and an intelligent driver to steer and control it. Your body has similar requirements; the Five Principles of yoga were developed by Swami Vishnu-devananda to fulfil them.

PROPER BREATHING
The breath links your body to its battery, the **solar plexus**, where potential energy is stored. The breathing techniques of **pranayama** release this energy for physical and mental rejuvenation.

PROPER RELAXATION
Relaxation acts as the body's cooling system. When your body and mind are overworked, their efficiency decreases. Proper Relaxation recharges them, releases all tension, and allows you to make the most of your energy.

• **FEET**
Starting with your feet and moving upward, consciously relax every muscle and joint in your body.

• **FRESH FOOD**
Fruit and vegetables
are vital elements in
a healthy diet.

PROPER DIET
The diet recommended in yoga philosophy
consists of simple, natural foods that are
easily digested and promote good physical
and mental health. Ideally vegetarian, it
includes fruits, vegetables, grains, leaves,
dairy produce, nuts, and seeds.

TORSO •
Try to hold your
trunk straight and
upright for this
balancing **asana**.

THOUGHT AND MEDITATION
Positive Thought and **Meditation** enable you
to become a good "driver". Positive Thought
purifies your intellect and gives you conscious
control over your instincts. Meditation puts
you in touch with your innermost being.

PROPER EXERCISE
In yoga this takes the form of **asanas**. These
"lubricate" your body, improving circulation
and flexibility. Asanas are unlike the violent
movements in most other types of exercise,
which may actually worsen fatigue.

SPACE & CLOTHES

Creating a comfortable environment for your yoga sessions

YOU WILL NEED a minimum of equipment to begin your practice of
yoga. It is the ideal method of exercise to learn at home. You may
choose to practise inside or, when the weather is fine, you may
prefer to do your yoga session in the fresh air. If you are outdoors,
find a location that is relaxing and secluded enough for you to
practise undisturbed. For yoga you do not need to buy expensive,
specially designed clothing. Dress simply and comfortably – try
a leotard or loose-fitting exercise clothes, so that your movements
are not constricted and you are not too hot or too cold.

A PLACE TO PRACTISE

For practising indoors, you will need
a clear space with no furniture. The
room should be comfortably heated
and well ventilated. It is important
to choose a place that is free from
disturbances and distractions. If the
room has no carpet, a rug or a folded
blanket can be placed on the floor.

CUSHIONS •
You may want to sit on a
cushion during **meditation**
and for the breathing and
preliminary exercises.

• TOWEL
A rolled up towel can be used
as an aid in **asanas** such as the
Cow's Head. (See p.58.)

RUG •
A rug can be placed on the
ground if you do not have a
carpet covering the floor.

BLANKET •
Wrap yourself in a blanket
during periods of relaxation,
as your body temperature will
drop while you are resting.

WHAT TO WEAR

You do not need any special clothing for yoga, but what you wear must be comfortable and allow the maximum range of movement. It is best to wear items made from natural materials. If you have long hair tie it back, so that it does not interfere with your **asanas**. Keep a sweater to hand in case you start to feel cold.

T-SHIRT •
A loose-fitting cotton
T-shirt is ideal wear
for yoga sessions.

TROUSERS •
Comfortable tracksuit
bottoms or trousers are
suitable and inexpensive.

LEOTARD •
A leotard is not essential, but
it will allow you freedom of
movement. Choose one made
from a stretch cotton mix.

WARMTH

Keeping warm during a session is
essential. A small electric heater can
help to keep the room in which you
practise at a comfortable temperature.

• FEET
Do not wear shoes for yoga, as they
will restrict your foot movements.
Bare feet are preferable, but if you
are cold you can wear socks.

YOU & YOUR BODY

Understanding how your body works and is constructed

BEFORE YOU EMBARK on your yoga course, it is wise to become
familiar with your physical make-up. The body is a remarkable
machine, consisting of a strong skeletal structure supported by
flexible muscles and ligaments. Your muscles have a dual role: they
hold you steady when you are in a particular position, and by
extending and flexing they allow you to move your body. In order
to work most efficiently, they must be long enough to permit the
free movement of your joints, as well as short and strong enough to
provide postural stability. Yoga **asanas** exercise your body naturally,
stretching each of its muscles slowly and taking into account its
limitations and capabilities. Regular yoga practice enables you to use
your joints to the full, enhances flexibility in your limbs and spine,
and results in the correct alignment of your skeletal frame.

MOVEMENT

The cycle of **asanas** (see pp.22-23) is
designed to contract and extend your
muscle groups in the right order.
To tone your muscles, you flex
certain groups fully while
letting the opposite
muscle groups
extend as far
as possible.

EXTENSION
Muscles need to be able to stretch, to allow
free movement. The Forward Bend shown
here fully extends the hamstrings and the
back muscles.

SPINE
The **vertebrae** from the **lumbar**
to the **cervical** region of the
spine are stretched in this pose.

ABDOMEN
As the muscles of the spine flex
in the Bow, their opposites, the
abdominals, are extended.

CONTRACTION
In this pose, the muscles extended in the
Forward Bend are contracted, stretching the
opposing group of muscles in the abdomen.

KNOW YOUR BODY

Stress, poor posture, and spending too long sitting or standing can all put a strain on your body. If you know your basic anatomy, you will be able to focus on problem areas, and so derive the most benefit from your **asanas**.

Deltoids lift and rotate arm

Pectorals pull in and rotate arm

Intercostal muscles expand the chest

Scapula (shoulderblade)
Sternum (breastbone)
Ribs
Ulna
Radius
Pelvis

Femur
Patella
Tibia
Fibula

Rectus abdominis supports abdomen

Sartorius twists thigh and bends hip and knee

Tibialis anterior raises foot

THE BODY'S FRAME
The skeleton is the body's frame; 206 bones support fat and muscle tissues, and protect vital organs such as the lungs, heart, and brain.

MUSCLES
Muscles support and move the body. They act in groups to bend the joints or hold the skeletal frame steady.

YOGA & YOU

Yoga is for everyone, young and old. It is different from other forms of exercise in that yoga **asanas** are intended to bring about a harmonious balance in your body and your mind. While there is no one who should be categorically exempted from doing yoga exercises, consult your doctor before beginning a course if you suffer from any medical condition or if you have any doubts. This book is designed as an introduction to the classical teachings of yoga; if you wish to learn more about this discipline, and to attempt more difficult asanas, it is best to work with a qualified teacher. If the exercises shown in the course are practised in the right spirit, they can be of great benefit to both mind and body. Remember, however, that yoga alone is in no way meant to be used as a medical prescription for any condition.

STRONG & SUPPLE

Tests to determine your muscular strength and flexibility

A HEALTHY BODY is both flexible and strong. The object of yoga is to balance suppleness with strength; regular practice allows these qualities to be maintained. Although none of us can avoid becoming less mobile as we grow older, poor posture and lack of exercise often hasten the process. For example, sitting hunched over desks or steering wheels for too long can cause tension in your back muscles and rounding of your chest and shoulders. The following tests will help you to locate areas of weakness and stiffness in your body.

MUSCLE STRENGTH

Your muscles must be strong enough to keep your body stable when you are standing or in any other pose. If they are weak, you will suffer from bad posture and limited joint movement. Using the information provided by the following tests, you can focus on **asanas** that will strengthen particular areas of weakness in your body.

OFF THE GROUND
This exercise tests your upper abdominal muscles. Lie on your front, with a partner holding your feet so that they do not lift off the floor. Then bend your arms up, arch your back, and raise your body as high as possible.

PELVIS •
Arch your spine upward from your pelvis.

• FEET
Lift your feet as high as possible.

LIFT YOUR LEGS
Lie on your back. Try to lift both legs so that they are at 90° to your body, while keeping your **lumbar** area flat. Any arching of your back indicates weakness in your abdominal muscles.

MUSCLE FLEXIBILITY

Muscles must be long enough to allow free joint movement. The following tests will reveal any limited joint motion. During your yoga sessions, gently try to stretch tight muscles. Do not attempt to compensate for stiffness by overstretching your more flexible muscles.

LEGS UP STRAIGHT
Lie on your back, and let a friend lift one of your legs as high as possible. Keep both legs straight. If your hamstring is tight, your leg will not rise far. Tight **lumbar** muscles will make your back arch.

HIPS •
Bend forward from your hips.

LEGS •
Keep your legs straight but relax your muscles.

TOUCH YOUR TOES
Sit with your spine and legs straight, then lean forward and try to touch your toes. This exercise will help you to feel the length of your back muscles, your hamstrings, and the muscles at the back of your calves.

BEND YOUR SPINE
Lie face down with your arms by your sides. Keeping your legs straight, ask a friend to lift your feet as high as possible. This exercise shows up stiffness in your back and in the muscles at the front of your chest.

PROPER BREATHING

Understanding and enhancing your breathing capability

TO LIVE IS TO BREATHE. Without oxygen, no cell in your body would be able to live for more than a few minutes. Most people use only a fraction of their full breathing capacity. This inefficiency allows fatigue and stress to set in. Proper breathing can tone up your entire system and enhance health and vitality. **Pranayama** breathing exercises are the link between the physical and mental disciplines of yoga. In all these exercises exhalation, rather than inhalation, is accentuated. This is because correct exhalation cleanses the lungs and speeds the elimination of toxins from your body.

BREATH AWARENESS

Understanding the mechanics of your lungs

THE MECHANICS

During yoga **asanas**, you breathe through your nose. When you inhale, your **diaphragm** moves downward and air is drawn into your lungs via your trachea and bronchial tubes. When you exhale, your diaphragm moves upward and pushes the air out of your lungs.

TRACHEA •
Air is drawn down your trachea to the lungs.

LUNGS •
Your lungs are protected within your ribcage.

DIAPHRAGM •
This provides 75% of the movement in respiration.

INHALATION
Your intercostal muscles and **diaphragm** stretch, and this pulls air into your lungs.

EXHALATION
As the **diaphragm** moves upward again, the air is pushed out of the lungs.

LYING DOWN

The following exercises teach you to breathe efficiently. Lie flat on your back. Put one hand on your abdomen. Breathe slowly and gently; feel your abdomen rise as you inhale and fall as you exhale. Keep your breathing slow, deep, and relaxed. This movement is important, as it brings air to the lowest and largest portion of your lungs.

USING YOUR DIAPHRAGM
Deep abdominal breathing exercises the **diaphragm**. Proper use of this muscle can greatly enhance your breathing capacity.

• LEGS
Your legs are relaxed, as is the rest of your body.

• HAND
Rest one hand on your abdomen, and feel it move as you breathe.

SITTING UP

HEAD •
Your head is erect and in line with your body.

Sit up straight, placing one hand on your abdomen and the other on your lower ribcage. Imagine that you can see your lungs. First, draw air into the lowest part of your lungs. Next, pull air into the middle of your lungs by stretching your intercostal muscles. Finally, feel the upper portion of your lungs expand. Most people breathe too shallowly, using only the upper part of their lungs; this practice is known as clavicular breathing, and ideally should be avoided.

• RIBCAGE
If you lay one hand on your ribcage, you will feel it expand as your muscles stretch it.

• ABDOMEN
As your lungs start to fill with air, feel your abdomen expanding.

BREATHING EXERCISES

*An introduction to **pranayama** – yoga breathing*

SINGLE NOSTRIL

Close your right nostril with your right thumb. Exhale completely through the left. Inhale to a count of 4, then exhale to a count of 8. Repeat 5 times. Close your left nostril with your ring and little fingers. Breathe through your right nostril, using the method given above. Repeat 5 times.

RIGHT HAND •
Your right hand assumes
Vishnu Mudra.

LEGS •
Your legs are crossed in
the **Easy Pose**, and your
back is straight.

MUDRA
For **Vishnu Mudra**, extend your thumb, ring finger, and little finger, and fold down your other 2 fingers.

– CUSHION COMFORT –

To keep a comfortable, straight pose, sit with a cushion under your buttocks when performing **pranayama**.

START TO ALTERNATE

When you are comfortable with Single Nostril Breathing, try breathing with alternate nostrils, as shown below, for a few rounds. Next, inhale with one nostril, but this time exhale with the other. Start a round by inhaling with the left nostril. Close it with your hand, then exhale right. Inhale right, close your right nostril, and exhale left. Do 10 of these rounds daily.

1. INHALE
Inhale with your left nostril to a count of 4.

2. EXHALE
Exhale through this nostril to a count of 8.

3. INHALE
Inhale with your right nostril to a count of 4.

4. EXHALE
Exhale through this nostril to a count of 8.

ALTERNATE NOSTRIL

When you are comfortable with the preliminaries, begin full Alternate Nostril Breathing. Holding your right hand in **Vishnu Mudra**, close your right nostril with your thumb. Exhale fully through the left, then go through 1 round as shown. Try to perform at least 10 rounds daily for best results.

1. INHALE
Inhale with your left nostril to a count of 4.

2. RETAIN
Close both nostrils; hold to a count of 16.

3. EXHALE
Exhale through the right, to a count of 8.

4. INHALE
Inhale through the right, to a count of 4.

5. RETAIN
Again, close nostrils for a count of 16.

6. EXHALE
Exhale through the left, to a count of 8.

KAPALABHATI

Kapalabhati, which means "shining skull", is believed to give the face an inner radiance. Sit cross-legged. Relax by taking a few deep breaths. Inhale deeply, then follow the steps below. Do 25 rapid pumpings in each round, and relax between rounds with a few deep breaths. Try to do at least 3 rounds before going on to the **asanas**.

• **FACE**
Relax your face. Keep your mouth closed, and breathe through your nose.

• **STRAIGHT**
Keep your torso straight and do not lean forward.

1. AIR OUT
Pull in your abdominal muscles forcefully, as though you have been punched in the belly. Your **diaphragm** will move up quickly, and this will push the air out of your lungs.

2. AIR IN
To take in air, relax your abdominal muscles and let your **diaphragm** descend. Do not force the inhalation.

THE SEQUENCE OF ASANAS

*Introducing the yoga **asanas***

SHOWN HERE IS THE sequence of **asanas** covered in the Weekend Course. Each asana or cycle of asanas prepares the body for the next pose. To derive the maximum benefit from this course, it is suggested that you do the sequence in the order specified here. The first pose taught is the Headstand, the "king of asanas". Next come the forward bends and their counterposes. These exercises are followed by the backward bends. The session ends with the lateral stretches and standing poses. Following the full programme will balance, strengthen, and tone your entire body.

*The Headstand
(pp.34-37)*

*The Shoulderstand
(pp.38-39)*

*The Plough
(p.40)*

THE HEADSTAND
One of the most famous poses, this is the first full **asana** taught during the Weekend Course.

SHOULDER POSES
In the Shoulder cycle, your spine is bent forward. The Fish, which follows, bends your spine backward.

*The Fish
(pp.42-43)*

*The Forward Bend
(p.46)*

FORWARD BENDING
This seated pose stretches your upper body forward. It also extends the muscles in the backs of your legs.

BACK BENDS
After bending forward you move on to the backward bends. Each vertebra is given a stretch in these vital **asanas**.

The Cobra
(pp.50-51)

The Locust
(pp.56-57)

The Bow
(pp.54-55)

SPINAL TWISTS
After stretching your spine backward and forward, you give it a lateral twist in this **asana**.

The Spinal Twist
(pp.60-61)

The Crow
(pp.62-63)

BALANCING POSES
The Crow improves your concentration and strengthens your forearms.

Hands-to-Feet
(p.66)

STANDING
The Hands-to-Feet and the Triangle, in the standing cycle, work every part of your body.

The Triangle
(pp.67-69)

THE WEEKEND COURSE

Introducing your weekend yoga course

YOUR WEEKEND COURSE HAS fifteen skills spread over two days. On the first day, you are introduced to the warm-ups and the inverted and sitting poses. Day two involves reviewing the **asanas** learnt in the previous day, then going on to the remaining poses. The skills are presented in the correct order, so you may wish to try part of each on day one. If you feel that covering all these poses in two days is too much for you, build up your practice more slowly. Try not to strain yourself, and do not omit the relaxation periods.

The Butterfly (pp.48-49)

DAY 1		Minutes	Page
SKILL 1	Opening a session	20	26-27
SKILL 2	The Sun Salutation	20	28-31
SKILL 3	Leg raises	10	32-33
SKILL 4	The Headstand	10	34-37
SKILL 5	The Shoulder cycle	20	38-43
SKILL 6	The Fish	10	44-45
SKILL 7	Bend & straighten	10	46-47
SKILL 8	Sitting poses	20	48-49

The Shoulderstand (pp.38-39)

KEY TO SYMBOLS

CLOCKS
Each skill is accompanied by an image of a clock. This shows the approximate time needed to assimilate and attempt the skill. The time is measured in minutes; blue sections indicate the number of minutes that have been allocated to the skill, and grey sections show you how much time has already been used on the course. The times given are only guidelines, though, and you may need to spend more or less time than suggested on a particular **asana**.

••••• RATING SYSTEM
All the skills are given ratings, to show the degree of difficulty involved. These ratings are indicated using bullets. One (•) denotes a straightforward skill that may be easily attempted by a beginner. Skills that are given five bullets (•••••) may be more complex, and you could require more practice before you attempt them. Some of the skills are divided into more than one pose; where this is the case, ratings are supplied for each **asana** in addition to the skill as a whole.

Final relaxation
(pp.72-73)

The Sun Salutation (pp.28-31)

DAY 2		Minutes	Page
SKILL 9	Stretching back	20	50-53
SKILL 10	Back bends	25	54-57
SKILL 11	Joint mobility	15	58-59
SKILL 12	Spinal twisting	10	60-61
SKILL 13	Balancing poses	15	62-65
SKILL 14	Standing asanas	20	66-71
SKILL 15	Final relaxation	15	72-73

Triangle variations
(pp.68-69)

Hands-to-Feet
(pp.66-67)

1

OPENING
A SESSION

DAY 1

Definition: *Mental and physical preparation for your session*

TO ENSURE THAT MAXIMUM BENEFIT is obtained from **asanas**, rest
in the **Corpse Pose** for at least five minutes before proceeding with
a session. In between asanas it is essential that you relax, breathing
deeply, so the Corpse is also held for a short time between poses,
and for longer at the end of each session (see pp.72-73). At the start
of a session you also perform shoulder, neck, and eye exercises in
the **Easy Pose,** a sitting posture that supports your back.

OBJECTIVE: Complete relaxation. *Rating* •

THE CORPSE POSE

Lie on your back and close your eyes.
Shake out your shoulders. Turn your
head from side to side, then return it
to the centre. Stay still, and take 10
deep breaths. Focus on your breath
so that it becomes very gentle, with
a slow and regular rhythm. Your
heart rate will also
slow to its resting level.

• **ARMS**
Place your arms so that
they are at a 45° angle
to your body.

• **BREATHING**
Breathe using your abdomen.
Feel it rise with each inhalation,
and sink with each exhalation.

FACE •
Remember to relax
your face and keep
your eyes closed.

• **FEET**
Place your feet 60cm
(2ft) apart, so that
your toes fall out.

FINGERS •
Let your fingers curl
slightly. Keep your
hands relaxed, with
your palms upward.

HEAD •
Sit straight,
keeping your
head, neck,
and trunk
aligned.

THE EASY POSE

The **Easy Pose** is a simple cross-
legged position, often adopted
naturally when sitting on the
floor. In yoga, it is one of the
basic positions used during
meditation, breathing, and
warm-ups. Sit upright and
keep your spine straight
so that it gives your
body firm support.

FOR COMFORT
Sitting on a cushion
keeps you straight
and eases pressure
on your knees.

• HANDS
Place your hands so that
they rest on your knees.

NECK ROLLS

Practise each set of neck rolls 3 times,
returning your head to the centre
between exercises. Sit in the **Easy
Pose**. In the first exercise, bend your
neck forward slowly, hold for a few
moments, then bend it back. In the
second, tilt your head right, hold, then
tilt it left. In the third, look over your
right shoulder, hold, then look over
your left. Finally, rotate your head.

HEAD •
Rotate your
head clockwise
3 times and
anticlockwise
3 times.

EXERCISING YOUR EYES

Making circles (above). Palming (right)

• Move only your eyes in these exercises.
Relax them in between. Unless another
number is specified, do each 10 times.
• To begin, look up and then look down.
• Open your eyes wide. Look from right
to left, then from left to right, and finish
by looking diagonally.
• Move your eyes in
circles. Start slowly,
and increase speed. Do
this movement 5 times
in each direction.
• Close your eyes. Rub
your hands together so
that they feel warm.
Cup them over your
eyes for 30 seconds.

SKILL

2

THE SUN SALUTATION

DAY 1

Definition: *A twelve-part warm-up exercise*

PERFORMED AT THE START of every **asana** session, each of the 12 positions of The Sun Salutation brings a different **vertebral** movement to your spinal column. Initially, just learn the physical movements. Once you have mastered these, tune them to your breathing. Do not start a session without doing this sequence.

OBJECTIVE: Preliminary limbering up.   *Rating* •

—————— Steps 1 & 2 ——————
STANDING

From the starting pose, below, exhale as you put your palms together at chest level. This first stance, called the Prayer Pose, centres your body. Next, inhale as you stretch your arms over your head and arch your back into the second position. Your hips come forward, and your head tilts back.

STARTING
Stand straight. Bring your feet together and hold your arms by your sides. Take a deep breath, and begin the Sun Salutation.

ARMS •
Keep your elbows straight, and align your arms with your ears.

KNEES •
Keep your knees straight, but do not lock them.

FEET •
Place your feet together. Balance your body weight evenly on them.

Steps 3 & 4
OVER & OUT

Exhale as you stretch forward and down into the third position. Place your hands on the ground so that your fingers and toes form a straight line. Bend your knees if necessary, but keep your hips held high. To assume the fourth position, inhale as you stretch your right leg back and bend your knee to the ground.

HEAD •
Stretch your head right back and look upward.

• FOREHEAD
Tuck your forehead in to your knees.

FEET •
Keep your feet close together.

• HANDS
Keep your hands on the ground on either side of your feet.

Steps 5 & 6
FACING THE FLOOR

For position 5, hold your breath as you bring your left foot back next to your right. Your body will be in a press-up position. Try to align your head with your neck and back, so that your spine is straight. Exhale into position 6, lowering your knees to the floor and laying your chest down between your hands.

HIPS •
Take care not to drop or raise your hips.

ELBOWS •
Keep your elbows straight when you are in the press-up position.

KNEES •
Allow your knees to touch the ground.

HIPS •
Your hips are raised up off the ground.

FOREHEAD •
Your head is tilted so that your forehead touches the floor.

Steps 7 & 8
BACK & FORWARD

For position 7, inhale as you slide forward
and lower your hips. Arch your chest and
lean your head back. Exhale into position
8. Put your feet flat on the floor, and lift
your body into an "Inverted-V".

SHOULDERS •
Your shoulders
are back and
relaxed.

ARMS •
Bend your arms slightly and
bring them in to your body.

• ELBOWS
Straighten your elbows when
you come into this position.

• HANDS
Maintain the flat
hand position of
the previous step.

• HEELS
Stretch your heels
toward the ground.

Steps 9 & 10
COMING TO A CLOSE

Position 9 is a mirror image of the
fourth position. Inhale, moving your
right foot forward. Keep your left
knee down, and look up. Next,
exhale into position 10; put
both feet together, stretch
your hips up, and tuck
your head in.

• HIPS
Keep your hips
stretching up.

KNEE •
Drop your back
knee to the ground.

FINGERS •
Your fingers remain
in line with your toes.

• **ARMS**
Hold your arms next to your ears, keeping your elbows straight.

— Steps 11 & 12 —
FULL CIRCLE

Inhale into position 11, stretching your arms up and arching backward as for position 2. For the final pose, exhale as you straighten up and lower your hands to your sides. Keep your body straight and relaxed. Take a deep breath to prepare for the next Sun Salutation. This is like the first, but your opposite leg leads. Once you have mastered the sequence, try to tune the moves to your breathing.

LEGS •
Keep your knees straight and your feet together.

FEET •
Keep your feet together.

GREETING THE SUN

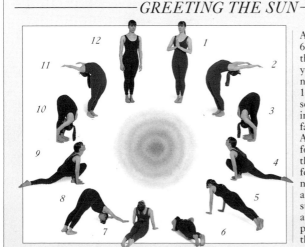

Attempt to do at least 6 Sun Salutations at the beginning of every yoga session. The ideal number to perform is 12. Traditionally, the sequence is practised in the morning, while facing the rising sun. As well as preparing you for the ensuing **asanas**, the sequence creates a feeling of harmony with nature. Move smoothly and gracefully. Make sure that you do not do any variations of the poses, as this will break the momentum.

SKILL

3

LEG RAISES

Definition: *Leg lifts performed lying on your back*

DAY 1

IN ORDER TO ENSURE THAT you obtain the maximum benefit from **asanas**, your body needs to become stronger as well as more flexible. The Sun Salutation has provided you with initial limbering up; practising the leg raises will develop your physical strength and make it easier for you to perform asanas correctly. These exercises are especially good for strengthening your abdominal and **lumbar** muscles. It is important to keep your back as flat as possible on the floor, and your shoulders and neck relaxed. If you are unable to lift your legs all the way up while keeping your back flat on the ground, raise your legs only as high as you can manage.

OBJECTIVE: To strengthen your abdominal and **lumbar** muscles. *Rating* •

SINGLE LEG RAISES

Lie on your back and put your feet together. Push your back into the ground to keep your spine straight, then inhale as you lift one leg as high as possible. Try to synchronize your movements with your breathing. To finish, exhale as you lower your leg.

• **BACK**
Keep your back pushed into the ground.

• **STRAIGHT**
Keep your foot straight as you raise your leg.

• **HANDS**
Lay your hands next to your body with the palms down.

EACH LEG
Begin by raising your legs individually. Lift each leg at least 3 times.

LEG STRETCHING

Inhale, raising one leg. Grasp it, and stretch it toward your head. Lift your head to your leg. Hold for 10 seconds. Exhale as you lower your head and your leg.

• HANDS
Use both hands to catch hold of your leg.

• HEAD
Raise your head as you grasp your leg.

WIND RELIEVING

Hug one knee to your chest, and raise your head up to your knee. Hold the pose for about 10 seconds. Exhale as you release your leg, straighten it, and lower it. Repeat the pose with your other leg.

STARTING POSE
As you inhale, bend one knee up to your chest, and hold it with both hands.

• KNEE
Your knee is as close to your chest as possible.

LOWER LEG •
Keep your lower leg close to the ground.

DOUBLE LEG RAISE

Lie with your feet together and your hands flat on the floor next to your body. Push your back down, breathe in, and raise both legs. Exhale as you lower your legs. Start with 5 raises, and build up to 10. If you cannot manage this exercise with your back flat, just do the single leg raises until your back becomes stronger.

BACK •
Ensure that your back does not arch upward.

• NECK
Push the base of your neck into the floor.

4

THE
HEADSTAND

Definition: *An **asana** in which you balance on your elbows, arms, and head*

KNOWN AS THE "KING OF **ASANAS**" because of its many benefits, the Headstand is the first of the 12 basic asanas and is considered by many to be a panacea for countless human ills. Sitting and standing for most of the day causes your circulation to become sluggish, so your heart has to work harder to pump sufficient blood to the upper parts of your body. Normally, your heart works against gravity; inverting your entire body lessens the strain on your heart, and allows a plentiful supply of oxygen-rich blood to reach your head and brain. This pose is not an advanced asana; even so, to begin with you may wish just to undertake the **Child's Pose** and the Dolphin, progressing to the full Headstand later.

OBJECTIVE: To relax and invigorate your entire body. *Rating* ••••

THE CHILD'S POSE

This is another relaxation pose, and is practised before the Headstand and some other **asanas**. Sit on your heels, then bring your forehead forward to rest on the ground. While in this pose, relax in order to prepare yourself mentally for the Headstand.

HANDS
Lay your hands on the floor beside your feet, with the palms upward.

BUTTOCKS •
Bend forward from your hips, but make sure that your buttocks stay resting comfortably on your heels.

FOREHEAD •
Let your forehead touch the ground.

PROTECTION •
For comfort, you can use a rug or a mat during the Headstand.

THE DOLPHIN

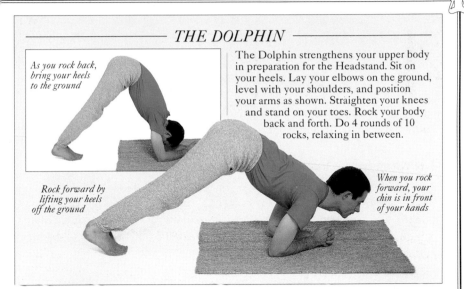

As you rock back, bring your heels to the ground

The Dolphin strengthens your upper body in preparation for the Headstand. Sit on your heels. Lay your elbows on the ground, level with your shoulders, and position your arms as shown. Straighten your knees and stand on your toes. Rock your body back and forth. Do 4 rounds of 10 rocks, relaxing in between.

Rock forward by lifting your heels off the ground

When you rock forward, your chin is in front of your hands

Step 1
ARMS & HANDS

Sit up on your heels, then catch hold of both your elbows with the opposite hands. Lean forward and lay your forearms on the ground, directly beneath your shoulders. Let go of your elbows, and clasp your hands together.

TRIPOD
Interlock your fingers to form a cap for your head to rest against.

• **ELBOWS**
Focus both weight and thought on your elbows.

Step 2
HEAD DOWN

HEAD REST
Rest your head in your hands.

With your arms in the tripod position, above right, lower your head so that the top of your skull touches the ground and the back of it is cradled in your hands. Do not make any abrupt movements. Take the next steps slowly.

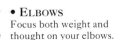

• **WEIGHT**
Little of your weight is on your head.

SKILL
4

——— Step 3 ———
ON YOUR TOES

From the crouched position with your head resting in your hands, straighten your knees and push your hips up above your head. Then, keeping your legs straight, stretch up high on your toes.

HIPS •
Keep your back straight and your hips directly over your head.

WALK IN
Walk your toes in toward your head. Do not drop your hips or bend your knees.

——— Step 4 ———
HALF HEADSTAND

Now bend your knees, bringing them to your chest. Arch your back slightly, as you do when standing up; this will enable you to balance your body in this position. Do not proceed unless you can hold this position for at least 30 seconds without feeling any discomfort.

KNEES •
Bring your knees in to your chest.

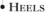

• HEELS
Your heels remain tucked in close to your buttocks.

• ARCH
Do not arch your back too much. It should keep the natural curve that it has when you stand upright.

——— Step 5 ———
KNEES UP

With your knees still bent, start to straighten your hips. Slowly and carefully, raise your knees until they are pointing straight up toward the ceiling.

ELBOWS •
Rest your weight on your elbows.

FEET •
Stretch your feet up, keeping them flat and parallel to the ceiling.

KNEES •
Keep your knees straight, and do not allow your legs to drop back.

HIPS •
Hold your hips straight above your head.

MUSCLES •
Tighten your abdominal muscles. This maintains correct posture, and prevents your back from arching too much.

Step 6

ALL THE WAY

Straighten your knees and lift your feet up toward the ceiling. Support your weight by bracing your elbows against the ground. At first, hold the Headstand for 30 seconds; as you become more skilled at adopting this pose, gradually increase the time to 3 minutes. Always come down before you start to feel tired. Leave the pose slowly and under control (see box).

HEAD IN HANDS
Rest the back of your head against your hands. Relax, breathing through your nose.

• WEIGHT
Throughout the **asana**, keep most of your weight on your forearms and elbows, rather than on your head.

COMING OUT

You should leave this **asana** as carefully as you entered it. Do not move jerkily or quickly, or you may lose control and fall.
• Bend your knees and lower them.
• Straighten your legs. Bring your feet to the ground, and then lower your knees.
• Lower your body so that your buttocks rest on your heels as in the **Child's Pose**.

• Finally, relax your hands and return to the full Child's Pose.
• Do not lift your head up straight away. Rest for at least a minute.
• Relax in the **Corpse** before continuing.

Legs down (above). Feet to floor (right)

5 THE SHOULDER CYCLE

Definition: *Postures in which you balance on your shoulders*

SARVANGASAN, THE **SANSKRIT** NAME FOR the Shoulderstand, comes from the word "sarva", meaning whole. This **asana** strengthens your entire body; it gives many of the benefits of the Headstand, but here the circulation is directed to your thyroid gland instead of your brain. The Plough follows on from the Shoulderstand, and gives similar benefits. The cycle ends with the Bridge, which counters the two previous poses. All three improve the flexibility of your spine.

OBJECTIVE: To stretch your **cervical** and **thoracic** regions. *Rating* •••

THE SHOULDERSTAND

An inverted pose, with your body resting on your shoulders. Rating •

— Step 1 —
LEGS IN THE AIR

Before beginning the Shoulderstand, make sure that there is enough room behind you. You must be able to stretch your arms out behind your head and have at least 30cm (1ft) between your fingertips and any obstructions. Lie flat on your back, with your feet together. Inhale while bringing your legs up to a right angle.

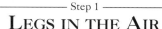

• **LEGS**
Bring both legs up at a right angle to the ground.

• **BREATHING**
Breathe in as you raise your legs.

HANDS •
Lay your hands flat on the floor next to your sides.

• **BACK**
Keep your back flat on the floor.

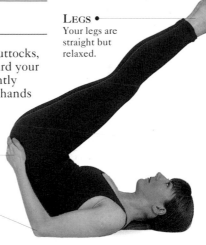

Step 2
MOVING UP

Tuck your hands under your buttocks, with your fingers pointing toward your spine. Then, as you exhale, gently raise your body by letting your hands walk down your back and push you into position.

LEGS •
Your legs are straight but relaxed.

HANDS •
Your hands form a support for your back.

ELBOWS •
Your elbows are bent and flat on the floor.

Step 3
IN BALANCE

Continue to move your hands up your back until you rest on your shoulders. Breathe normally, and keep your legs straight. Hold for 30 seconds; as the pose becomes easier, increase the time to 3 minutes. To come down, drop your feet halfway to the floor behind your head. Put your hands on the floor. Unroll your body **vertebra** by vertebra to the floor.

HAND POSITION
Put your hands on the small of your back, with your fingers toward your spine.

FEET •
Keep your feet close together.

• HANDS
Support your body weight evenly with both your palms.

VARIATION
Inhale with your hands on your back. Exhale and bring one foot to the floor behind your head. Inhale. Raise your leg. Swap sides.

NECK •
Feel your body lift from the base of your neck. Press your chin into your neck.

5

THE PLOUGH

On your shoulders with your feet behind your head. Rating ••

——— Step 1 ———
LEGS OVER

In the Plough, your body is bent forward; this stretches your entire spine, particularly your **cervical vertebrae** and shoulders. Come up into a Shoulderstand, and inhale deeply. Exhale while lowering your feet to the floor behind your head.

• LEGS
Stretch your legs over your head.

UPPER BACK •
The Plough helps to make your upper back more flexible, nourishing your spinal nerves.

——— Step 2 ———
LEGS DOWN

Rest your toes on the floor, then lay your arms down flat. Hold for 30 seconds at first, but aim to build up to 2 minutes. If you cannot lower your feet all the way, keep your hands on your back for support. To come out, lift your feet off the floor, and slowly roll down. Relax in the **Corpse**.

HANDS
Lay your hands flat on the floor, palms downward.

HEELS •
Push your heels back, as if trying to bring them to the ground.

PLOUGH VARIATION

You may try this variation if you are supple enough. Once in the Plough, lower your knees to the floor by your ears. Hook your arms over your legs. To come out, straighten your knees, then roll down as described above.

• KNEES
Bend your knees to the floor.

ARMS •
Hook your arms over your knees.

THE BRIDGE

Arching up with your head, shoulders, and feet on the ground. Rating •••

Step 1
ON YOUR BACK

Done straight after the Plough, the Bridge is a complementary stretch for your **thoracic** and **lumbar** regions, releasing any muscle tension that has built up. From the **Corpse Pose**, bend your knees and lay your feet on the floor by your buttocks.

STARTING POSE
Relax in the **Corpse Pose** before you attempt the Bridge.

FEET •
Your feet are positioned close to your buttocks.

Step 2
ARCH UP

Place your hands flat on your back, with your fingers pointing in toward your spine, as for the Shoulderstand. Keeping your head, shoulders, and feet on the floor, arch your hips and chest up as high as possible. Hold the position for 30 seconds.

• **FEET**
Keep your feet flat on the floor.

• **FINGERS AND THUMBS**
Your fingers point toward your spine, and your thumbs toward the ceiling.

BRIDGE VARIATION

Once you are supple enough, try this variation. Come into the Bridge, inhale, and raise one leg, keeping it straight. Exhale as you lower it. Repeat the pose with both legs, holding each leg in the air for a few seconds before lowering it.

• **LEGS**
Lift your leg up above your head, keeping it straight.

FOOT •
One foot stays flat on the floor to help support your weight.

THE FULL SEQUENCE

Putting together all three poses. Rating •••

COMBINING THE POSES

Once you have mastered the Shoulderstand, Plough, and Bridge, and feel comfortable in each position, all three **asanas** can be linked to form an uninterrupted sequence. The full series of poses is shown here.

• **KNEES**
Keep your knees straight as you lift your legs.

HIPS •
Your hips are aligned with your shoulders.

• **BACK**
Your back stays flat on the floor as you lift your legs.

STARTING
Begin the sequence by lying flat on your back and lifting your legs and body into the Shoulderstand. Hold this position for 3 minutes.

THE PLOUGH
Lower your legs as shown on the left, and come into the Plough position. Hold the pose for 2 minutes, then return to the Shoulderstand for a further 30 seconds.

• **LEGS**
Your legs stay straight as you lower them.

FEET •
Your feet touch the floor.

• FEET
Lower your feet slowly, one at a time.

DOWN TO THE BRIDGE
While in the Shoulderstand, bend one leg and lower your foot to the ground, then lower the other leg. Arch your back, and push your hips upward. Do not change your hand position; if you feel pressure on your wrists, push your elbows wider apart.

• HIPS
Your hips are pushed upward.

LEGS •
Kick your legs quickly up into this position.

BACK UP AND RELAX
Inhale deeply, and kick one leg and then the other back up to the Shoulderstand. Next, lower both your feet halfway to the floor behind your head. Lay your arms on the floor behind your back, then slowly roll out of the pose. To finish, relax in the **Corpse Pose**.

• CHEST
Breathe normally while in the pose.

SKILL

6

THE FISH

DAY 2

Definition: Lying on your back and arching your chest

THE FISH IS THE STRETCH that counters the Shoulderstand and Plough, and so follows them in a yoga session. The name of the posture derives from the fact that if you adopt the position in water, you will float quite easily. The **asana** does wonders for your respiratory system; when you assume this position, your chest is stretched open and your bronchial tubes are widened to promote easier breathing. In time your ribcage will expand, and this will also encourage you to breathe more deeply. By lifting your chest and tucking your arms underneath your body, you will combat postural defects such as rounded shoulders. In addition, the Fish removes stiffness from your shoulders and the **cervical** region of your spine, thus releasing pressure on your nerves. Try to hold the pose for half of the time that you spent in the Shoulderstand, in order to equalize the stretching effects on your spine and muscles.

OBJECTIVE: To ease tension and improve spinal flexibility. *Rating* •

––––––––––– Step 1 –––––––––––

ON YOUR BACK

Assume the **Corpse Pose** and, when you are ready, begin to come into the Fish. Stay flat on your back, and bring your feet together. With your arms straight by your sides, lay your palms on the floor, then tuck your hands in underneath your buttocks.

STARTING POSE
Prepare yourself for this **asana** by relaxing in the **Corpse Pose** for as long as you need.

• **FEET**
Lie with your feet together and toes pointing upward.

HANDS •
Keeping your arms straight, put your hands under your buttocks.

HEAD •
Begin with your head upward.

CHEST LIFT
Press your elbows down on the floor, inhale, and arch your chest upward as far as you can.

HEAD BACK

Having arched your spine, tilt your head so that your crown rests on the ground. Hold for 30 seconds. To come out of the Fish, slide your head back and then lower your chest. To finish, relax by lying in the **Corpse**.

LEGS •
Your legs are straight but stay relaxed.

FISH VARIATION

Try this variation if you are flexible enough. In the **Easy Pose**, clasp your toes. Lie back, arch up, and rest your buttocks on your heels. Lay the top of your head on the floor.

HANDS •
Your hands hold on to your toes.

• **CHEST**
Your chest arches up as much as possible.

KNEES BENT
Sit cross-legged, then put your arms down behind your knees and catch hold of your toes.

FISH IN LOTUS

This pose is an advanced variation on the ordinary Fish. It is similar to the **Easy Pose** variation shown above, except that it begins with the Lotus (see p.49). Practitioners of yoga use this variation for staying afloat in water. The Fish in Lotus pose should not be attempted by beginners, or even by more experienced yoga students, until the full Lotus position can be held comfortably for a long period of time.

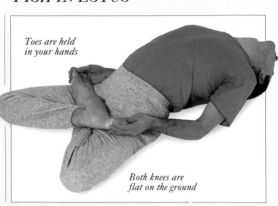

Toes are held in your hands

Both knees are flat on the ground

7

BEND & STRAIGHTEN

Definition: *Stretching your spine forward*

THE FORWARD BEND LOOKS, AND IS, SIMPLE – provided you relax into the position, rather than forcing yourself into it. The pose is one of the most powerful and important **asanas**, helping to ease the spinal compression caused by standing upright. Its practice contributes greatly toward keeping your back supple, your joints mobile, your nervous system invigorated, and your internal organs toned. The Inclined Plane is the counterpose to the Forward Bend. It complements the forward stretch that your body is given in the previous pose, and increases the strength and flexibility of your arms. In this **asana** your hips are pushed upward, and your body is held straight and balanced on your hands and feet.

OBJECTIVE: To stretch the back of your body. *Rating* •

FORWARD BEND

Lean forward from your hips, and try to catch hold of your toes. Keep your spine and legs straight. Exhale into the pose; feel your body stretch. Hold for 30 seconds, then inhale and stretch upward again. Repeat twice.

STARTING
Inhale, bringing both arms up by your ears. Stretch your spine up.

• **CHEST**
Bring your chest as close to your thighs as you can manage.

• **HEAD**
Lower your head to your knees, but do not force it down.

CLASP POSITION
If you are unable to reach your toes, clasp your ankles, shins, or knees, to hold the position comfortably.

INCLINED PLANE

From the starting position below, let your head drop back. Next, inhale as you raise your hips. Hold the pose for about 10 seconds. Lower your body, then relax your hands by shaking your wrists.

• **HEAD**
Hold your head back.

• **FEET**
Your feet are together and flat on the floor.

STARTING
Sit with your legs straight. Put your hands flat on the floor behind you.

• **JOINTS**
Keep your knees straight and your hips up as you hold this pose.

FIRST VARIATION

At this point, you can lie back and relax in the **Corpse**. However, if you are strong enough, you can try some variations on the pose. For the first, lift one leg up, hold for a few seconds, and then slowly lower it. Repeat the position on both sides.

SECOND VARIATION

For this position, come up into the Inclined Plane, and then raise one arm. Hold for a few seconds, then lower your arm to the ground. Repeat the position, alternating the arm that you raise.

• **ARMS**
All of these poses strengthen your arms.

SKILL

8 SITTING POSES

DAY 1

Definition: Exercises performed while seated

MANY PEOPLE TODAY spend a lot of time sitting hunched in chairs. This shortens and weakens their back muscles. The seated poses featured here can help to remedy poor posture brought on by such inactivity. This lesson closes the first day; remember to finish by relaxing in the **Corpse Pose**, as you should after every yoga session.

OBJECTIVE: To stretch your back muscles. *Rating* ••••

ONE KNEE BENT

STARTING POSE
Sit with straight legs. Put one foot against your other thigh, then inhale as you lift your arms straight up.

Assume the starting pose, and stretch your spine up as far as you can. Then exhale while bending forward over your straight leg, and grasp your toes. Hold for 30 seconds. Inhale as you come up. Repeat with the other leg.

• **SPINE**
Keep your spine as straight as you can manage.

CHEST •
Bring your chest down to lie on your leg.

FEET APART

Sit with your legs wide apart. Inhale as you lift your arms over your head, then exhale as you stretch forward. Grasp your toes, and lower your head toward the ground.

• **NECK**
Relax your neck, letting your head hang down.

FEET •
Catch hold of your feet with your hands.

THE BUTTERFLY

Sit up straight, bend both knees, and bring the soles of your feet together. Next, catch hold of your feet with both hands and draw them in close to your body, then gently bounce your knees down toward the ground. Make sure that your hands are holding your feet firmly, and that your feet are as close to your body as possible.

TORSO •
Keep your torso straight and upright.

FOOT UP
Alternate your upper foot in the Half Lotus.

HANDS •
Rest your hands gently on your knees.

THE HALF LOTUS

Bring one foot up to rest on the opposite thigh. Tuck your other foot under your upper thigh. This pose is known as the Half Lotus. If you are supple enough, you can use it instead of the **Easy Pose** during your breathing and warming up exercises.

THE LOTUS POSE –

The Full Lotus is an advanced position, which should not be attempted until you have been practising yoga for some time, and have mastered all of the other seated poses shown here. This classic pose involves resting the backs of both feet high up on their opposite thighs.
The lotus flower is a significant symbol in the culture and mythology of India. The plant has its roots in mud, but the flower constantly strives to lift its head toward the light of the sun. Unaffected by the mire from which it rises, the lotus is considered beautiful because of this struggle. In yoga it represents self-awareness, and its namesake is adopted for **meditation** and breathing exercises.

SKILL

9 STRETCHING BACK

DAY 2

Definition: *Asanas to stretch your spine backward*

THE COBRA AND LOCUST are the first two new poses for day two. Before attempting them, remember to do the breathing exercises, preparation for the session, and the Sun Salutation, followed by the poses covered on day one. The Cobra is a face-down position in which you lift your upper body. The pose works both the deep and the superficial muscles of your back, toning and strengthening the abdomen. In the Locust you lift your lower body, working your back muscles and stimulating your internal organs.

OBJECTIVE: To increase flexibility in your spinal column. *Rating* •••

THE COBRA

Coiling your upper body up and back. Rating •••

—————— Step 1 ——————
FACE DOWN

Lie on your front in the **Corpse Pose** for at least 2 minutes. Then, when you are fully relaxed, begin to come into the Cobra. Still lying on your front, place your hands flat on the floor so that they are directly underneath your shoulders. Next, lift your head up a little and bend your neck, then lower your forehead to the ground.

STARTING POSE
Relax in the frontal **Corpse Pose** (see p.54). Lie on your abdomen, then place one hand on top of the other to make a pillow. Turn your head and rest your cheek on your hands.

• **FEET**
Place your feet with toes together and heels apart.

ELBOWS •
Tuck your elbows in close to your body.

HEAD •
Rest your forehead on the ground.

------------ Step 2 ------------
ROLL UP

Inhale, slowly rolling up and back. First, bring your forehead up, so that your nose rests on the floor. Next, raise your nose, then continue to roll up and back. Move slowly, so that you feel each **vertebra** arching back.

• ABDOMEN
Your abdomen remains in contact with the ground throughout this pose.

• SHOULDERS
Ensure that you do not hunch your shoulders.

LEGS •
Your legs stay straight and flat on the ground.

BACK •
Your back is arched, and your chest stretches out.

HOLD
Hold the pose for 10 seconds. Slowly roll down, keeping your head back until last. Repeat 3 times.

GOING FURTHER

Once you are proficient in the above steps, you can attempt some variations.
• In the Cobra, turn your head to look over your right shoulder, trying to see your left heel. Hold for about 10 seconds, then return your head to the centre and repeat while looking over the other shoulder.
• From the starting position, lift your hands off the ground and roll your body up using only your back muscles.
• Always return to a resting position on your abdomen after these poses.
• With practice you may be able to attempt the variation shown here, in which your feet touch your head.

SKILL
9

THE LOCUST

Lying face down with lifted legs. Rating ●●●●

— Step 1 —
FACE DOWN

Lie on your front. Rest your chin on the ground, then move it forward as much as you can, so that your throat lies almost flat. Put your arms by your sides, then push your hands under your body, and make them into fists or clasp them together. Bring your elbows as close together as possible.

STARTING POSE
Begin in the frontal **Corpse** (see p.54).

HEAD •
Stretch your head forward.

CLENCH
To help you lever your body upward, clench your fists together and push against the ground with your hands.

CLASP
You may find that clasping your hands together is more comfortable or that it allows better leverage.

— Step 2 —
HALF LOCUST

Inhale as you lift one leg. Hold this position for at least 10 seconds, then exhale while lowering your leg and repeat the pose with your other leg. Practise it 3 times on each side.

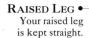

RAISED LEG •
Your raised leg is kept straight.

LOWER LEG •
Ensure that your lower leg remains flat on the floor.

HIPS •
Do not let your hips twist as you raise your leg.

CHIN
The further forward you push your chin, the more your spine can stretch and the more you will gain from this **asana**.

Step 3

FULL LOCUST

Lie with your chin out, as in the Half
Locust, then take 3 deep breaths. On
the third, lift both legs off the ground.
They may not come up far at first, but
with practice you may be able to lift
them much higher. Hold for as long
as you can, then lower your feet.
Repeat twice and then relax.

• FEET
Place your
feet together.

KNEES •
Hold your knees
straight, and raise
your legs as high
as you can.

• CHIN
Rest your chin
on the ground.

ELBOWS •
Keep your elbows
close together.

UP AND UP
With practice, you will
be able to raise your
legs higher. Eventually,
you may even be able to
lift your body vertically.

THE ADVANCED LOCUST

This more difficult pose
must be attempted only
by experienced students
of yoga. The aim, in the
advanced **asana**, is to
raise your feet straight up
and then lower them over
your head. This backward
bend compresses your
vertebrae while stretching
the front of your body to
its greatest extent. The
strength and flexibility
necessary for this pose
will eventually develop
with regular practice.

*Push your hands
down against the
floor for leverage*

10 BACK BENDS

Definition: *Backward bending poses*

TO KEEP YOUR BODY HEALTHY, your back must be strong and supple, with the ability to bend backward as well as forward. In other words, it should be balanced. The Bow works all parts of your back simultaneously. In this **asana**, your head, chest, and legs are lifted, while your body rests on your abdomen. The pose is so named because as you hold it, your body is bent back like a bow and your arms are held straight and taut like a bowstring. Initially, you may wish to attempt only the first 3 steps, moving on to the Rocking Bow when you have become more confident and lithe. The Wheel and its variations may appear difficult, but when worked on systematically they can bring both strength and flexibility to your spine and back muscles. All of these poses combine and augment the benefits gained from the Cobra and the Locust.

OBJECTIVE: To increase flexibility in your spine and hips. *Rating* ••••

FRONTAL CORPSE

Before and after all **asanas** you must relax for as long as necessary. The position that you adopt for relaxing between back bends is a variation on the **Corpse Pose**, in which you lie on your front. Like all Corpse variations, this pose prepares you mentally and physically for performing an asana.

HEAD ON HANDS
Your hands make a pillow on which you can rest your head as you relax in this position.

FEET
Position your feet with your big toes together; let your heels and ankles fall gently out to either side.

• ABDOMEN
Focus all your thoughts on your abdomen, while breathing deeply.

HEAD •
Rest your head first on one side and then on the other.

THE BOW

Balancing on your abdomen, in the shape of a bow. Rating •••

—— Step 1 ——
CATCH HOLD

To begin, lie on your front with your forehead on the ground. Now bend your knees and catch hold of your ankles. Make sure that you do grasp your ankles rather than the top of your feet or your toes. Keep your feet relaxed.

ARMS •
Keep your elbows straight.

HEAD •
Your forehead touches the ground as you begin the Bow.

—— Step 2 ——
LIFT UP

Inhale, raising your head, chest, and legs. Straighten your knees. Hold for 10 seconds, aiming to increase to 30. Breathe as you hold the pose. Exhale, and lower your body. Repeat 3 times.

• CHEST
Lift your chest as high as you can.

GRIP
Hold your ankles firmly as you rock.

ROCKING BOW

For this exercise, come into the Bow, arching as high as you can. Keep your head back and gently rock, using your breath to propel your body. Exhale as you rock forward, and inhale as you rock back. Do not forget to relax in the **Corpse Pose** on your front after you have completed this movement.

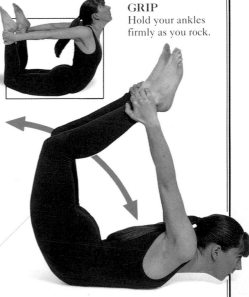

LEGS •
Lift your legs and hips up as high from the ground as possible.

10 WHEEL POSES

Auxiliary exercises to give your spine a full backward bend. Rating ••••

THE HALF WHEEL

Lying flat on your back, bend your knees and put your feet flat on the ground, near your buttocks. Grasp your ankles and push your hips up. Hold for 20 seconds. Practise until the pose comes easily before you go on to try the full Wheel.

STARTING
Lie on your back, then put your feet flat on the ground.

HANDS •
Your hands clasp your ankles.

• SHOULDERS
Your shoulders must stay on the ground during this pose.

———— Step 1 ————
STARTING POSE

Lie on your back, then bend your legs and put your feet by your buttocks. Bend your arms, and turn your hands so that your fingers point toward your shoulder blades. Lay your hands flat on the floor behind your shoulders.

HANDS •
Your hands lie flat on the ground, with your fingers pointing at your feet.

• KNEES
Straighten your knees as much as you are able.

———— Step 2 ————
INTO THE WHEEL

Lift your hips, arching your entire spine up and dropping your head back. In the full Wheel, only your hands and feet remain on the ground. Aim to hold the pose for 30 seconds. Your hands and feet will be parallel.

• HANDS
Walk your hands in toward your feet.

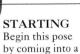

Step 1
KNEEL & LEAN

To assume the Camel, a pose also
known as the Kneeling Wheel, start
by sitting on your heels. Place both
hands behind your body and, resting
on them, drop your head back. Raise
your hips, arching them forward.

STARTING
Begin this pose
by coming into a
kneeling position.

HIPS •
Begin with your hips
and buttocks resting
on your heels.

• HANDS
Your hands are
placed flat on the
ground, pointing
backward.

• HEAD
Lean your
head back.

Step 2
INTO THE CAMEL

Walk your hands in toward your feet,
and try to catch hold of your heels. At
the same time, push your hips up and
forward as far as possible, and allow
your head to drop back. If this pose
is done correctly, your body will take
on a shape resembling a rectangle.

• HANDS AND HEELS
Move your hands toward your feet until
you are able to take hold of your heels.

THE DIAMOND

The advanced variation on
the Wheel is known as the
Diamond, and should only
be attempted when you
are able to hold the Wheel
easily. In this pose your
body forms the shape of a
diamond, hence the name.
The aim is to bend your
spine backward until your
head touches the floor,
then grasp your feet with
your hands. The pose is
completed by pulling with
your hands so that your
head comes down to rest
on top of your heels.

SKILL

11 JOINT MOBILITY

Definition: *Stretches for your shoulders and hips*

IT IS SAID THAT PEOPLE in the modern world carry the majority of their tension in their shoulders. This stress leads to problems such as hunched shoulders and stiff necks, which result in pain and excessive strain on the body. The Cow's Head and its variations relieve stiffness in your chest, neck, and upper back region. Practising these **asanas**, and their counterpose, the Frog, opens your chest and straightens rounded shoulders. The poses also enhance mobility and flexibility in your leg muscles and joints.

OBJECTIVE: To bring flexibility to your joints. *Rating* ••••

THE COW'S HEAD

Sit up on your heels. Bring your right arm over your head, bending your elbow. Put your left arm behind your back and clasp your hands. In this position, bend forward. Hold for 30 seconds and then sit up on your heels, releasing your hands. Shake out your arms and repeat on the other side.

TOWEL
If you cannot join your hands, hold a rolled towel behind you, gripping one end with each hand.

HANDS •
Keep your hands clasped while you are in this pose.

BUTTOCKS •
Sit with your buttocks resting on your heels.

HEAD TO FLOOR
To complete this **asana**, try to bring your forehead down as close to the floor as you can manage.

THE WARRIOR

Kneel, then drop your buttocks to the
floor between your legs. Cross your
right leg over your left, and tuck the
left underneath. Clasp
your hands as in the
Cow's Head. Hold
for 30 seconds,
then repeat the
pose with the
other elbow and
leg uppermost.

• ELBOW
Point your
upper elbow
at the ceiling.

FOOT •
Your lower foot
tucks in by the
top of your
other thigh.

• LEG
Your top leg rests
on your other leg.

• SPINE
Keep your spine
straight while you
are in this pose.

THE FROG

Begin in a kneeling position. Now
move your knees as far apart as you
can, while keeping your toes together.
Put your hands on the floor in front of
you, and walk them away from your
body. Straighten your arms, and lower
your trunk. Hold for 30 seconds.

• TORSO
Keep your torso
straight as you
bend forward.

BUTTOCKS •
Keep your buttocks
resting on your feet.

FINAL POSITION
Your torso rests on the floor, with
your arms straight in front of you.

SKILL

12 SPINAL TWISTING

DAY 2

Definition: *A lateral stretch for your entire spine*

AFTER BENDING FORWARD AND BACK, your spine requires a lateral twist to retain its mobility. This ability to twist is often the first type of flexibility to be lost. During the Spinal Twists your **vertebrae** are mobilized; the exercises also allow more nourishment to reach the roots of the spinal nerves and the **sympathetic nervous system**.

OBJECTIVE: To maintain sideways mobility in your spine. *Rating* •

Step 1
ONE LEG STRAIGHT

Relax in the **Child's Pose** before starting, then sit up with your legs straight in front of you. Bend your right knee, and put your right foot on the ground on the outside of your left knee.

• RIGHT LEG
Your right leg is bent and crosses over your left thigh.

• LEFT LEG
Your left leg is straight out in front of you.

ARMS
Place your right hand flat behind you. Raise your left arm in the air.

BUTTOCKS •
Both buttocks stay on the ground.

Step 2
TWIST ROUND

Twist to the right. Lower your left arm in front of your knee, and grip your right ankle. Look over your right shoulder. Hold for 30 seconds, then repeat on the left side.

STARTING
To begin, kneel
with your heels
tucked under
your buttocks.

LEGS BENT

This type of spinal twist, in which
both your legs are bent, should not
be attempted until you can hold the
previous pose comfortably. Sit up
on your heels. Drop your buttocks
to the floor, to the left of your legs.

• **HIPS**
Move your hips so that your
buttocks rest by your legs.

LEG POSITION

Bend your right leg. Cross your
right foot over your left leg, and
place it on the floor by the outside
of your left knee. Keeping your
arm straight, put your right hand
flat on the floor behind your back.

STRAIGHT BACK •
Keep your back straight
and upright.

ARMS
Lay your right hand
on the floor. Raise
your left arm
straight up.

HEAD •
Look over
your right
shoulder.

THE TWIST

Lower your left arm, bringing
it outside your bent knee, then
grasp your right ankle. Hold for
at least 30 seconds. Repeat,
twisting the other way.

SHOULDERS •
Twist your
shoulders
as much as
possible.

BUTTOCKS •
Both buttocks
stay resting on
the ground.

HAND •
Catch hold of your
ankle with your
opposite hand.

SKILL

13 BALANCING POSES

Definition: *Balancing your entire body on your hands*

ALL **ASANAS** SERVE TO IMPROVE physical and mental health, and increase your ability to focus the mind. Balancing exercises are particularly beneficial. Both of the poses shown here enhance concentration. The first pose, the Crow, develops mental tranquillity and also strengthens your wrists and forearms. The second, called the Peacock, demands a strong, flexible body and a disciplined mind. In this asana your elbows are bent into your abdomen. This allows a fresh supply of blood to the area, nourishing and toning your internal organs and eliminating sluggishness.

OBJECTIVE: To improve balance and concentration. *Rating* •••••

THE CROW

Balancing in a squatting position. Rating ••••

—————— Step 1 ——————
SQUAT TO START

To prepare yourself for the Crow, squat with your feet and knees wide apart. Position your arms between your knees, with your hands directly under your shoulders, then put your hands flat on the floor in front of you.

HANDS
Stretch your fingers wide and turn your hands inward slightly.

• KNEES
Bring your knees as far apart as you can comfortably manage.

FEET •
Lift your heels and rest your weight on the balls of your feet.

— Step 2 —
KNEES TO ARMS

Bend your elbows, and turn them
outward. Rest your knees against
your upper arms. Next, rock forward
until you feel your weight on your
wrists. Stay in this position if you
are unable to proceed further.

• EYES
Keep your eyes focused
on a point in front of you.

WEIGHT
This exercise is still
useful even if you
stop at this point, as
your wrists support
your weight and your
forearm muscles are
being stretched.

— Step 3 —
RAISE YOUR FEET

Slowly raise each foot, then balance
on your hands for at least 10 seconds.
Aim to increase your time in the pose
to 30 seconds; with practice you will
be able to hold the position for up to
a minute. To come out, lower your
feet to the ground, sit up, and shake
out your wrists. If you are strong
enough, repeat the Crow twice.

HEAD •
Ensure that your head
stays up. If it drops, you will
be more likely to roll forward.

• KNEES
Your knees rest
against your
upper arms.

• HANDS
Your hands and
wrists support
your weight.

• FEET
Your feet are held
in midair, with your
toes pointing down.

— PROTECTION —

FEAR OF FALLING
If you are worried about falling onto
your face, put a cushion in front of you.

SKILL
13

THE PEACOCK
Balancing with your body parallel to the ground. Rating •••••

• **TORSO**
Sit up, keeping
your torso straight
and relaxed.

Steps 1 & 2

HANDS TO THE FLOOR

Start in a kneeling position, then
move your knees apart. Place your
arms between your legs, bringing
your elbows and forearms together
and tucking your elbows in close
to your abdomen. Next, lay
your hands flat on the floor,
with your wrists together
and your fingers pointing
back toward your body.

• **FOREARMS**
Your forearms are
almost at right
angles to the floor.

STARTING POSE
Sit on your heels with
your knees wide apart.

Steps 3 & 4

STRETCH OUT

Keep your hands directly under
your abdomen. Put your
forehead on the ground.
Next, stretch one leg and
then the other straight
out behind you. Your
weight should now be
resting on your hands,
toes, and forehead.

HEAD •
Your forehead
touches the floor.

LEGS •
Stretch your legs straight
out behind you, supporting
them with your toes.

TOUCHING THE GROUND
At this point you are resting your weight
on your hands, toes, and forehead.

Steps 5 & 6
IN THE AIR

Raise your head, and shift your weight forward. Lift your toes. If you perform the movements slowly, you will raise your legs without effort. Hold for 10 seconds. With practice, you will be able to hold the pose for up to 30 seconds.

ARMS •
Your elbows are together and your weight is on your wrists.

EYES •
Focus your eyes on a point ahead to aid concentration.

• LEGS
Your legs are held straight and parallel to the ground.

PARALLEL BODY
In the final position, your body is held straight and parallel to the floor.

THE ADVANCED PEACOCK

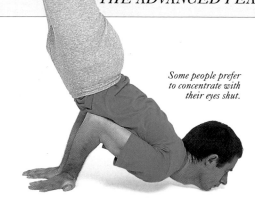

Some people prefer to concentrate with their eyes shut.

With practice, you may be able to try this variation on the Peacock. The pose does, however, call for a great deal of strength and agility, and must only be attempted by advanced yoga students. Such people may even find this version of the Peacock easier than the ordinary **asana**, as the legs are in balance with the body rather than hanging behind it. In this pose, you balance on your hands and chin, with your legs raised vertically behind you.

SKILL

14

STANDING ASANAS

Definition: *Poses practised in an upright position*

STANDING POSES DEVELOP strength and flexibility in your legs and hips, and equilibrium in your body. The Hands-to-Feet Pose stretches your spine and joints, and increases the blood supply to your brain. The Triangle is the last of the basic **asanas**. You must master this pose and its variations before trying the advanced asanas.

OBJECTIVE: To make your spine and legs supple and strong. *Rating* ••

HANDS-TO-FEET

Bending forward in a standing position. Rating •

FORWARD & DOWN

This is similar to the Forward Bend, but here gravity helps to stretch your body down. Stand with your feet together. Inhale, while lifting your arms straight above your head. Exhale as you bend forward and down. Breathe normally while you are in the pose. Hold for at least 30 seconds; as you gain experience, increase the time to several minutes.

LEGS AND HIPS •
Keep your legs straight. Make sure that your hips are over your feet and do not move backward.

FEET •
Your weight is centred, and poised on the balls of your feet.

• **FOREHEAD**
Tuck your forehead in toward your legs as far as you can manage.

THE TRIANGLE

A lateral bend resembling a triangle. Rating ••

TO THE SIDE

The Triangle is a lateral stretch for your trunk muscles and spine, and makes your hips, legs, and shoulders more flexible. Stretch your right arm up, then bend to your left, sliding your left hand down your thigh. Do not twist your body. Hold for 30 seconds, working up to 2 minutes with practice. Inhale as you straighten up again. Repeat the pose on the other side.

INITIAL POSE
Stand up straight, and place your feet slightly more than shoulder width apart.

ARM •
Raise your arm straight up above your head.

• HAND
Put your lower hand on your thigh to balance you as you bend.

BODY LINE
Your body forms a straight line, parallel to the floor, from your waist to your fingertips.

• HEAD
Keep your head in alignment with your straight spine.

KNEE •
Keep your knees straight while in this position.

• HAND
Your hand slides down toward your ankle.

TRIANGLE VARIATIONS

SKILL

14

Further poses to stretch and balance your body. Rating ••

STRETCH UP

Stand with your feet apart, turn your
left foot out, and bend your left knee.
Next, bend to the left and put
your left hand down by your
instep. Then lift your right
arm straight above your
head, and look up.
Hold for 30 seconds.
Repeat, bending
to the right.

ARM •
Your arm is held
straight out and
aligned with the
side of your chest.

• HAND
Keep your hand
flat on the floor.

• LEG
Stretch your straight leg
out as much as possible.

FINGERS •
Your fingers are closed and your
hand points up at the ceiling.

TWIST & LOOK UP

Stand with your feet apart. Hold
your arms straight out at shoulder
level, then twist to the left and
put your right hand down outside
your left foot. Keep your chest
and arms aligned, with your left
arm straight up and your
shoulders at 90° to the
floor. Hold the pose
for 30 seconds. Then
repeat it, but this time
twist to the right.

• HEAD
Turn your head
toward your
upper hand.

• HAND
Lay your hand flat on the floor,
on the outside of your foot.

TO THE SIDE

Stand with your feet apart, then turn your left foot out and bend your left knee. Next, twist to the left and put your right hand down outside or on your left foot. Raise your left arm straight up over your head. Repeat the pose, turning to both sides.

• BODY
Your body twists so that your right leg is aligned with your left arm.

• FOOT
Your foot is turned out as far as you find comfortable.

HEAD •
Try to touch your knee or leg with your forehead.

HEAD-TO-KNEE

Stand with your feet apart and your hands clasped behind your back. Turn to one side, and exhale as you lower your forehead to your knee. Then lift your arms as far from your back as you can, and hold for 30 seconds. Inhale as you stand up. Repeat, turning to the other side.

A DEEP LUNGE

Stand with your feet wide apart and your left foot turned out. Clasp your hands behind your back. Next, bend from the hips and lower your head to the floor by that foot. Keep your right leg straight. Then lift your arms as high as you can, and hold for 30 seconds. Practise the pose on both sides.

ARMS •
Your arms are raised up and away from your back.

THE STANDING POSES

SKILL
14

During these exercises, you balance on one foot. Rating ••

BALANCING PRAYER

Stand on your left leg. Lift your arms over your head, and put your hands together. Keeping your body straight, lean forward and raise your right leg. Hold for 10 seconds, then swap legs.

MIND POWER
Concentration is essential. Keep your balance by focusing your mind on a fixed point in front of you.

ARMS •
Hold your arms straight, beside your ears.

RAISED LEG •
Raise your right leg up behind you, keeping your knee straight.

• **FOOT**
Catch hold of your raised foot and lift it outward.

• **STRAIGHT LEG**
Keep your left leg straight and at 90° to the ground.

THE LORD NATARAJA

Stand on your left leg and bend your right knee. Bring your foot up to your buttock, and catch hold of it. Try to straighten your right knee, lifting your foot as far away from your body as you can. Then raise your left arm beside your left ear, and hold this position. In **Sanskrit**, "Nataraja" means "King of Dancers". This is another name for the god **Siva**, who, it is believed, first taught the yoga **asanas**.

BODY •
As your right leg rises, your trunk, right thigh, and raised left arm all stay aligned.

• **LEG**
Make sure that the leg on which you balance is straight.

THE TREE

Balancing on one foot, with arms lifted above your head. Rating ••

--- Step 1 ---
FOOT TO THIGH

Balance on your left foot, and focus
your mind on a fixed point. Bend
your right knee, and put your foot
on your left thigh. With practice,
you will be able to put your foot
at the top of your
thigh in the Half
Lotus position.

STARTING
Stand straight. Focus
your eyes on a point
at eye level, such as
a spot on a wall.

FOOT •
Hold your
foot in place
with both
hands.

--- Step 2 ---
HANDS OVER HEAD

Lift your arms up, and put your
palms together. Hold the pose
for a minute. If you wish, try the
following exercise. Focus on a
spot in front of you. In your
mind, pull the spot in
to rest between your
eyebrows. Close your
eyes, but keep your
mind on this point.

• BREATHING
Breathe deeply while
holding this pose to calm
and focus your mind.

RAISED FOOT •
Keep the sole of your
raised foot flat against
your inner thigh.

• LEG
Balance on one foot,
and keep your knee
as straight as possible.

15 FINAL RELAXATION

Definition: *Conscious relaxation while in the Corpse Pose*

KNOWING HOW TO RELAX is a vital part of keeping your body fit. Relaxation is primarily a mental process, as all muscle movements are controlled by your subconscious mind. By sending a message to each part of the body to relax, you can consciously ease any tension.

Do not omit this final skill – it is an essential element in your session, and will enhance all of the benefits gained from the **asanas**.

OBJECTIVE: To allow energy released by the **asanas** to flow free. *Rating •*

HEAD TO TOE

Lie in the **Corpse Pose**. Tense and relax all your muscles as shown, and do the head rolls. Then, in your mind, tell every part of your body to relax, starting with each toe. Feel the relaxation moving up your body. Finally, relax your jaw and let your mouth open slightly. Relax the back of your throat, then your tongue and face muscles. Stay in this pose for at least 10 minutes after each session.

• FEET
Your feet are about 60cm (2ft) apart, with your toes turned out.

RAISE YOUR LEGS
Raise each leg 5cm (2in) from the ground, tense and release the muscles, and let it fall.

LIFT YOUR HIPS
Lift your buttocks, tense and relax them, and let them fall. Do the same with your chest.

TENSE UP
Shut your eyes tight and screw up all of your face muscles.

STRETCH OUT
Open your eyes and mouth wide. Stick your tongue out fully.

ROLL YOUR HEAD
Slowly roll your head once or twice, touching the ground with one ear and then the other, then bring it to rest with your face upward.

• ARMS
Lay your arms at 45° to your body.

• BREATHING
Let your breathing become slow and gentle.

HANDS •
Your hands lie with palms upward and fingers curling gently.

FOCUS ON HANDS
Lift each hand 5cm (2in). Make a fist, tense your arm, then relax your hand and let it fall.

—MIND & SLEEP—

• Slow breathing relaxes the mind. Make your breathing very gentle and quiet. Imagine that your mind is a deep, still lake with no ripples. You have no worries or fears. Soon you will feel a sense of inner peace; enter into that peace and become one with it.

• Once you have learnt to relax, you may find that you can put this skill to use at other times as well. For instance, if you have trouble falling asleep, lie in bed and mentally go through the steps of this guided relaxation.

• If you practise the **asanas** followed by the relaxation period, you may find that you need less sleep than before and wake up feeling refreshed. This is because these techniques help you to go more quickly into deep sleep, which is the most restful type of sleep.

AFTER THE WEEKEND

What to do now you have finished your basic course

·

YOU HAVE NOW COMPLETED your introduction to the techniques of yoga **asanas** and **pranayama**. You will benefit most if you keep up your initial momentum with regular practice. Try to practise daily. If you feel stiff, do not be deterred; the best way to ease this is by doing a gentle asana session. Set aside a time when you will not be disturbed – perhaps first thing in the morning, or later in the evening before you have eaten. It is advisable to continue under the guidance of a qualified teacher, as he or she will be able to correct and improve your technique. The skills in this book are basic tools that can enhance your life, promoting good health and a positive attitude.

ORGANIZING YOUR PRACTICE

Fitting yoga sessions into your daily life

HERE ARE THREE suggested sessions, of different durations, for your yoga programme. They include time allowed for **asanas** and time for relaxation between poses. Try the shorter routines when you are busy, but aim to do at least two full sessions per week for maximum benefit. Do not leave out the breathing exercises. If you are short of time, you can do them separately – for example, do the breathing in the morning and the asanas later on. If you have no time for any of the sessions, try to do at least six rounds of the Sun Salutation and a Headstand.

Breathing exercise

The Shoulderstand

	Fast	Average	Full
Relaxation	1 x 5 mins	1 x 5 mins	1 x 5 mins
Kapalabhati	3 x 1 min	3 x 1 min	3 x 1 min
Alternate nostril breathing	5 x ½ min	10 x ½ min	10 x ½ min
Preliminaries: neck & eyes	2 mins	5 mins	5 mins
The Sun Salutation	6 x ½ min	12 x ½ min	12 x ½ min
The Headstand	1 x 1 min	1 x 2 mins	1 x 3 mins
Leg raises	1½ mins	2 mins	2 mins
The Shoulderstand	1 x 1 min	1 x 2 mins	1 x 3 mins
The Plough	1 x ½ min	1 x ½ min	1 x 1 min
The Bridge	1 x ½ min	1 x ½ min	1 x ½ min
The Fish	1 x ½ min	1 x 1 min	1 x 1½ min
The Forward Bend	3 x 10 secs	3 x 20 secs	3 x ½ min

	35 mins	60 mins	90 mins
The Inclined Plane	1 x ½ min	1 x ½ min	1 x ½ min
Sitting poses		1 min	3 mins
The Cobra	2 x ½ min	3 x ½ min	3 x ½ min
The Half Locust		4 x 15 secs	4 x 15 secs
The Locust		2 x ½ min	2 x ½ min
The Bow		2 x ½ min	3 x ½ min
The Half Wheel			2 x ½ min
The Full Wheel			1 x 1 min
The Camel			3 x ½ min
The Cow's Head			2 x ½ min
The Frog			1 x 1 min
Spinal twisting	2 x ½ min	2 x ½ min	2 x 1 min
The Crow or Peacock		2 x ½ min	3 x ½ min
Hands-to-Feet	1 x ½ min	1 x 1 min	1 x 1 min
The Triangle	2 x ½ min	2 x ½ min	2 x ½ min
Triangle variations			2 x ½ min
The Tree			2 x 1 min
Standing asanas			3 x 1 min
Final relaxation	1 x 5 mins	1 x 10 mins	1 x 10 mins
Running Time	30 mins	53 mins	72 mins

The Bow

Hands-to-Feet

	35 mins	60 mins	90 mins
Total session time allocated with relaxation between asanas	35 mins	60 mins	90 mins

ADVANCED ASANAS

Further yoga postures that you can achieve with practice

THERE ARE SAID TO BE 84,000 different yoga **asanas**. With so many poses to choose from, you are unlikely ever to feel bored. Once you have mastered the basic asanas covered in The Weekend Course, you will be on the way to developing the flexibility, strength, and confidence needed to attempt some of the more advanced variations. The postures shown here are just a few examples of what you can hope to achieve. Some asanas may be possible after just a few months of lessons, while perfecting others may take you years of tuition and practice. Make your progress at your own individual rate; remember that you must never force yourself into difficult positions before your body is ready. Never attempt any of these poses unless you are receiving guidance from a qualified teacher.

LOWER LEG •
Your lower leg is bent in toward your body.

• HIPS
Your hips arch outward as your entire body bends.

THE PIGEON
This **asana** is so named because your chest is open and pushed forward like that of a pigeon. Your hands, raised foot, and head all come together in a powerful backward bend.

THE SCORPION
Once you can hold the Headstand easily, you may be able to attempt the Scorpion. This pose bends your spine fully, and improves your circulation.

• CHEST
Your chest opens out
as your body stretches
back in this pose.

THE CRESCENT MOON
As the name suggests, your body
takes the shape of a crescent moon. This
shape is often seen as the symbol of yoga.
In the Crescent Moon, you balance on your
rear knee and toes and your front foot. Your
arms and spine stretch backward.

LOWER LEG •
Your lower leg stretches
back as far as possible.

FRONT FOOT •
Keep your front foot flat
on the floor for balance.

THE TORTOISE
Your legs are wide apart and your body bends
down toward the floor. Your arms are tucked
under your legs. With practice, it is possible
to lay your chin and chest on the floor.

• ARMS
Your arms are tucked
underneath your thighs
in this forward bend.

THE PEACOCK IN LOTUS
In this variation on the Peacock, you balance
your body on your hands as in the basic pose.
This time, though, you start by crossing
your legs in the Lotus position before
you lift them off the ground.

FEET •
Your feet are tucked
up and rest on the
opposite thighs.

HANDS •
Your fingers are spread
out to take your weight.

GOOD FOOD

Planning a balanced and nutritious diet for your body and mind

WHATEVER FORM OF PHYSICAL EXERCISE you practise, a healthy diet will increase your energy. Plan your diet so that it includes all the essential minerals and vitamins, as well as plenty of carbohydrates, protein, and fibre. Keep your intake of fat down by trying to avoid meat, fried foods, and snacks such as chocolate and crisps. Instead, eat plenty of fresh vegetables and fruit, and foods such as grains, nuts, and seeds.

• **VEGETABLES**
Providing vitamins, minerals, and fibre, vegetables are both delicious and vital for a healthy diet. Eat them raw or lightly cooked to retain their natural goodness.

CARBOHYDRATES •
Great energy-givers, pasta and rice can be satisfying elements in your diet. Other carbohydrates that you can include are bread and potatoes.

— A YOGA DIET —

The ideal diet for yoga is essentially vegetarian. Yoga philosophy identifies three categories of food.
• **Sattvic**, or pure, foods are items such as fresh fruit, grains, and vegetables. These form the bulk of a yoga diet.
• **Tamasic** – rotten or stale – foods include alcohol, meat, and tobacco.
• **Rajasic**, or overstimulating, foods include hot spices, coffee, and tea.

JUICY FRUIT •
Sweet but healthy, fruit is an ideal snack. Most varieties are low in fat but still high in vitamins and minerals.

BREAD AND CHEESE •
Cheese and other dairy products contain calcium for strong teeth and bones. Brown bread provides fibre as well as carbohydrates.

NUTS AND SEEDS •
Nuts and seeds also contain protein. There are many kinds to choose from, and they make a convenient snack.

• **PULSES**
Pulses give concentrated protein. For vegetarians they are a useful, filling alternative to meat.

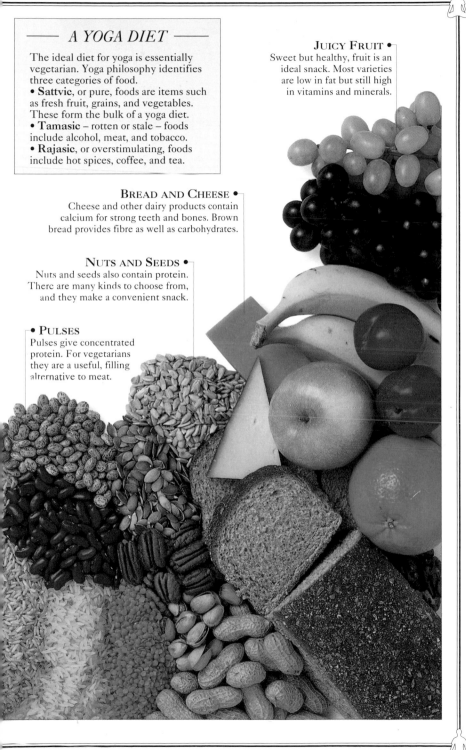

MEDITATION

Learning to focus and channel your mental energy

MEDITATION IS A STATE of consciousness; it allows you to go beyond the limits of normal awareness. Imagine that your mind resembles a lake. The bottom of the lake may be seen very clearly if the water is calm, but this will not be possible if the water is disturbed by waves. In the same way, when your mind is perfectly still you can bypass everyday distractions and perceive the source of true contentment. Meditation differs from deep sleep or relaxation in that it involves active mental effort rather than total rest. As well as relieving stress and replenishing energy, it can bring you physical, mental, and spiritual peace. To achieve inner serenity, you must learn to make your mind quiet and focus your mental energy inward. If you meditate for half an hour daily, your thinking will become clearer and you will be able to face life with greater spiritual strength.

AN IDEAL POSE

The ideal positions for meditation are the classic sitting postures, as these keep the **prana**, or vital energy, within your body. The Lotus, Half Lotus, and **Easy Pose** are all suitable. Place your hands in a comfortable position; some appropriate poses are shown here.

BREATHING •
Breathe quietly from your abdomen. Maintain a regular rhythm.

CHIN MUDRA
Form a circle with your thumb and first finger. Rest the backs of your wrists on your knees.

CUPPED
You can relax both hands in your lap, palms upward, one on top of the other.

CLASPED
You may also clasp your hands gently and lay them in your lap as you meditate.

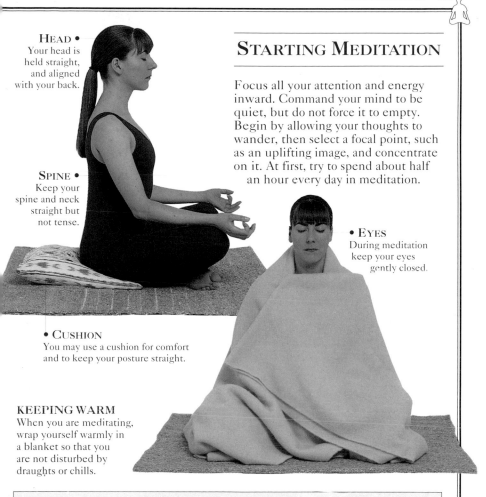

HEAD •
Your head is held straight, and aligned with your back.

SPINE •
Keep your spine and neck straight but not tense.

STARTING MEDITATION

Focus all your attention and energy inward. Command your mind to be quiet, but do not force it to empty. Begin by allowing your thoughts to wander, then select a focal point, such as an uplifting image, and concentrate on it. At first, try to spend about half an hour every day in meditation.

• EYES
During meditation keep your eyes gently closed.

• CUSHION
You may use a cushion for comfort and to keep your posture straight.

KEEPING WARM
When you are meditating, wrap yourself warmly in a blanket so that you are not disturbed by draughts or chills.

POINTS TO REMEMBER

• Always use the same time and place to meditate. This conditions your mind to become calm quickly. Set aside a special area. Do not let anything disturb you. At first, try to sit for 20-30 minutes daily.

• Start with 5 minutes of deep abdominal breathing. Then breathe gently, inhaling for 3 seconds and exhaling for 3 seconds.

• You may use a **chakra** as a focal point. If you have a rational nature, use the Ajna Chakra, between the eyebrows. If you are more emotional, use the Anahata Chakra, near the heart. Never change your chakra.

• You may use a **mantra**. Repeat it once as you inhale and once as you exhale. If you do not have a personal mantra, use **OM**.

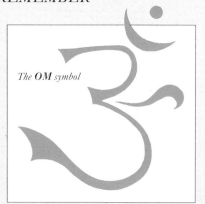

The OM symbol

HEALTH & LIFE

How the practice of yoga can aid some common ailments

IN ADDITION TO improving physical strength and flexibility, yoga can be helpful for those who suffer from specific complaints. While it is not regarded as a cure for physical or medical conditions, yoga can relieve many of them. Even for the fittest people, gentle physical exercise, combined with a healthy diet, can be very beneficial.

Meditation calms your mind

FOR YOUR HEALTH

Shown here are some yoga exercises that can help to relieve mental or physical problems. While these may be focused on, a full routine of **asanas** is suggested to keep the body strong and balanced.

The Cow's Head eases stiff shoulders

STRESS
Asanas make your body more flexible, and release tension. **Meditation** and breathing techniques also help to lower stress levels.

ASTHMA
Backward bending exercises such as the Fish relieve congestion in your chest, and breathing exercises can help to strengthen your respiratory system.

ARTHRITIS
Arthritis sufferers may find that focusing on the Cow's Head and the sitting cycle eases stiffness in the hips and shoulders.

The Fish opens up your chest

The Half Locust strengthens your lower back muscles

LOWER BACK PAIN
Single and double leg raises, and the Half Locust, will help to strengthen the muscles in your abdomen and your **lumbar** region. The Cobra and the Bow are also helpful, as they increase the flexibility of muscles in these areas.

PROPER POSTURE

Yoga promotes good posture, which relieves strain on your spine as well as improving your appearance. Imagine a line passing through the side of your body. If you are standing straight, your limbs, head, and **vertebrae** will be in alignment with this line. The images on the right show ideal posture.

HEAD •
Your head is aligned with your chest, hips, and feet.

CHEST •
Your chest is pulled upward and does not bow in or out.

ARMS •
Let your arms hang loosely by your sides.

ABDOMEN •
Your abdomen is flat and pulled in.

LEGS AND FEET •
The line passes behind your knee joint and through your foot.

FEET •
Balance your body weight evenly on both your feet.

SPINAL STRUCTURE

Cervical region

Thoracic region

Sacral region

Lumbar region

Coccyx

The spine has 29 **vertebrae**. At the neck are the 7 **cervical** vertebrae. Extending from the shoulders to the waist are the 12 | **thoracic** vertebrae. The lower part of the spine contains the 5 **lumbar** vertebrae, the 5 **sacral** vertebrae, and the **coccyx**.

YOGA FOR ALL

Yoga exercises for every stage of life

—•—

WHATEVER YOUR AGE, yoga can enhance your lifestyle. For instance, it can help teenagers to keep their youthful flexibility and give them the inner strength to say no to negative influences. Older people often find that gentle yoga exercises allow them to retain mobility, and may relieve problems such as arthritis and poor circulation. Everyone can benefit from following a regular yoga routine, as it counteracts many of the problems suffered in modern life. **Asanas** release the physical tensions caused by hours of sitting, **pranayama** gives vitality by increasing the supply of oxygen to the brain, and **meditation** enhances the powers of concentration. Yoga improves strength and flexibility in the mind as well as the body, and aids relaxation. It frees the practitioner both physically and mentally, often heightening intuition and creativity.

LATER YEARS

The gentle movements used in yoga are perfectly suited to older people, especially those with an interest in physical, mental, and spiritual growth. Regular practice allows elderly people to maintain their health and mobility. Yoga can enable one to relax fully, and promotes sound sleep; it also improves digestion, stimulates circulation, and eases arthritis.

FEET •
Gentle yoga exercises
improve circulation in
your feet and hands.

• HIPS
Stiffness in your
hips can be relieved
by some **asanas**.

CHILDREN

As well as being fun, learning yoga develops self-discipline in children and can enhance their physical and mental health. **Asanas** are good for developing coordination, and help to improve concentration and memory. Regular practice can enable young people to keep their natural flexibility for many years.

• **LEGS**
In the Triangle, your legs are placed wide apart to balance you while you stretch sideways.

PREGNANCY

Yoga promotes good health in both mother and unborn child. Yoga **asanas** lessen the effects of such problems as overweight, backache, and depression. Most women who practise yoga find that it can make labour easier and shorter. Although some asanas have to be modified during pregnancy, their essence is perfectly suited to this time of expanded self-awareness. Pregnancy is also a very good time for **meditation**.

CROSS-LEGGED •
This pose, which comes naturally to children, can be used in **meditation**.

• **ABDOMEN**
Many of the **asanas** can be adapted during pregnancy, as your abdomen gradually becomes larger.

YOGA & SPORT

How the practice of yoga can help other sporting interests

WHATEVER SPORT you choose to practise, yoga can enhance and complement your ability. Most sports build muscular strength and stamina, often in specific areas of the body. Yoga can help to check any imbalance in muscular development, and will enable both your body and your mind to function more efficiently. If your body is flexible and supple you will be less prone to sports injuries, as your joints will be kept lubricated. Although you can focus on particular poses to help you in your chosen sport, it is always more beneficial if you complete a whole **asana** session.

LIMBS •
Yoga makes your limbs balanced, strong, and relaxed.

GOLF
Golfers may be prone to one-sided or uneven muscle development. Yoga **asanas** can strengthen weak areas and ease muscular tension.

LEGS •
The standing poses improve balance and muscle flexibility.

SKIING
Skiing demands mental alertness as well as good balance. **Asanas** can strengthen your muscles, release physical tension, and improve your concentration and poise.

SWIMMING
Yoga breathing techniques help swimmers to breathe in a relaxed way when exercising. A full yoga session will improve flexibility.

BACK •
Back bends can relieve any stiffness caused by bending over handlebars.

• HIPS
Asanas for joint mobility can make hips and shoulders more flexible.

RACKET SPORTS
These often involve intense physical effort. Yoga practice can help players to relax and replenish their energy after strenuous games. It also promotes calm, clear thinking, even in situations that call for fast reactions.

CYCLING
Because a cyclist's back stays in one position for long periods, the muscles may become tense. This can be remedied with back bends and stretches. Gentle stretching exercises also ease stiffness in the legs and shoulders.

WHERE TO PRACTISE

*Stimulating and inspirational environments for your **asanas***

•

TO VARY YOUR YOGA PRACTICE, it is sometimes helpful to give your
mind a break from daily routine. Once you have mastered the skills
covered in this book, you may want to practise in more congenial
environments. Imagine spending a weekend, or a week, away from
it all on a secluded beach or mountain top. Your day may begin
with morning **meditation**, followed by **pranayama** and an **asana**
session to invigorate your body. A diet of simple, nutritious foods
will relax and strengthen you. If you go through your yoga routine
in such peaceful surroundings, you may come to feel that you
are in harmony with your inner self, humanity, and nature.

IN THE OPEN

Your yoga session can be done in any
surroundings. However, as yoga is
meant to balance your body and mind,
it is best practised in a natural setting
where there is very little activity.

MEDITATION IN A FOREST
Being in an unspoilt place such as a forest,
at a peaceful time such as sunrise, can make
meditation easier and more meaningful.

SUNSET ON A BEACH
Sunset is also a time of peace. Practising yoga
then, surrounded by the calm and beauty of
the ocean shore, can be highly beneficial.

ASHRAMS

An **ashram** is a special place set up for the teaching and daily practice of yoga. Such an environment can be a haven from the demands of everyday life, a place where you can **meditate**, relax, learn, exercise, and contact the peaceful centre within yourself. A stay at an ashram will give you a taste of the healthy, balanced lifestyle that can be achieved if you follow the Five Principles of Yoga, which are given on pp.10-11: proper exercise, breathing, relaxation, diet, and positive thought and meditation. Spending time at an ashram will give your life and your practice a boost. Here you will be provided with extra encouragement and energy, and this will help you afterwards when you continue with your daily yoga sessions.

COMMUNITY SPIRIT

Doing yoga exercises in a group, such as this one at the Sivananda **Ashram** Yoga Camp in Quebec, helps to develop community spirit.

PROPER INSTRUCTION

Proper instruction is important, as can be seen in this class at the Sivananda **Ashram** Yoga Retreat on Paradise Island, Nassau, Bahamas.

GLOSSARY

Words in *italic* are glossary entries.

A

• **Asana** A physical exercise in yoga, which is done to improve the control of body and mind. In *Sanskrit*, this word means posture, position, or seat.
• **Ashram** A peaceful retreat where yoga is taught and practised.

C

• **Cervical vertebrae** The top 7 *vertebrae* of the spine. These bones support your neck. By holding your head correctly, you maintain their natural curvature.
• **Chakras** The 7 centres of spiritual energy in the body. The highest chakra corresponds to the pineal gland, at the top of the head, and the others lie on a line corresponding to the spinal cord.
• **Child's Pose** A relaxation pose done before and after the Headstand, and between other *asanas*. In this pose you kneel, then bend forward so that your head rests on the ground.
• **Chin Mudra** See *Mudra*.
• **Coccyx** The small curved bone at the base of the spinal column.
• **Corpse Pose** The primary relaxation pose, this is done between *asanas* and at the end of a session. Usually you lie on your back, but during the back bending cycle the Corpse can be done while lying face down.

Kapalabhati can be done before an asana session

D

• **Diaphragm** The muscular partition between your lungs and your abdomen.

E

• **Easy Pose** A simple cross-legged pose that is used during warm-ups, *meditation*, and breathing exercises.

H

• **Hatha yoga** The word Hatha comes from the *Sanskrit* names for the sun and the moon, and indicates the union of opposites. Hatha yoga is the path of yoga that deals with the control of the body. The basics of this discipline are set out in the ancient scripture known as Hatha Yoga Pradipika. This work is said to have been written by the sage Swatmarama, as an inspiration from *Siva*, the first teacher of yoga.

K

• **Kapalabhati** An exercise involving rapid abdominal breathing, which is carried out to cleanse the respiratory tract. This is one of the 6 kriyas, or cleansing exercises.

L

• **Lumbar vertebrae** The lumbar group, in your lower back, consists of 5 *vertebrae*, and supports most of your body weight. This part of the spine is quite flexible. It takes on a slightly curved shape when you are standing upright or walking.

M

• **Mantra** A syllable, word, or phrase that is used to focus the mind during *meditation*. It is repeated either in your mind or aloud. The best known mantra is the syllable *Om*.
• **Meditation** A state of consciousness characterized by stillness and inner calm. The ultimate goal, in this practice, is the attainment of supreme spiritual peace.
• **Mudra** A hand position that allows the *prana* to be channelled in specific

directions. The hand positions that are featured in this book are *Chin Mudra* and *Vishnu Mudra*.

O

• **OM** This sacred syllable, sometimes written AUM, is the original *mantra*. The *Sanskrit* letter represents the journey of the human spirit toward eternal peace.

P

• **Prana** The vital energy or life force. It flows through the body along canals that are known as nadis.
• **Pranayama** Yogic breathing exercises designed for cleansing the body. In the more advanced stages, pranayama enables the practitioner to control the flow of *prana*, or vital energy, in the body.

R

• **Rajasic** The term that is used for overstimulating foods such as coffee and hot spices. These are governed by Rajas, the quality of nature that is active and restless. Rajasic foods are best avoided, as they put excessive stress on your body and mind.

S

• **Sacral vertebrae** These 5 *vertebrae* make up the lowest region of the spine. They are fused to form a single bone, which is part of the pelvic girdle.
• **Sanskrit** An ancient literary language of India.
• **Sattvic** A term used for the most wholesome foods. These are governed by Sattva, the quality of nature that is pure. Yoga practitioners usually keep to a sattvic diet, as this cleanses and invigorates the body and mind.
• **Siva** The divine inspiration for yoga. Most of the classical works on yoga are in the form of an exposition by Siva, the great yogi, to his wife Parvati.
• **Solar plexus** The network of nerves that lies just behind the stomach.
• **Sympathetic nervous system** This is part of the autonomic nervous system, which controls all involuntary muscle movements. It activates whole groups of muscles at once, in response to stimuli such as fear or excitement.

T

• **Tamasic** The word for overripe or stale foods. These are governed by Tamas, the quality of nature that is inert, and should be avoided as they cause lethargy and mental dullness.
• **Thoracic vertebrae** These are the 12 *vertebrae* in the chest area, to which the ribs are connected. This part of the spine tends to be rather rigid.

U

• **Upanishads** The ancient *Sanskrit* scriptures containing the central tenets of Hindu mysticism and philosophy.

V

• **Vedanta** The philosophy on which yoga theory is based.
• **Vertebrae** The 29 bones that form the spinal column.
• **Vishnu Mudra** See *Mudra*.

FURTHER READING
The Book of Yoga, Sivananda Yoga Centre, Ebury Press
The Complete Illustrated Book of Yoga, Swami Vishnu-devananda, Harmony Books
Hatha Yoga Pradipika with Commentary Swami Vishnu-devananda, Om Lotus Publishing
Science of Pranayama, Swami Sivananda, Divine Life Society
Sivananda Yoga Video with Training Manual, Sivananda Yoga Centre
Yoga Asanas, Swami Sivananda, Divine Life Society

Meditation is often practised in the Lotus position

INDEX

GETTING IN TOUCH

SIVANANDA YOGA
VEDANTA CENTRE
51 Felsham Road
London SW15 1AZ
Telephone: 081 780 0160

SIVANANDA ASHRAM YOGA
CAMP HEADQUARTERS
8th Av Val Morin
Quebec, Canada, JOT 2RO
Telephone: 819 322 3226

ACKNOWLEDGMENTS

The Sivananda Yoga Vedanta Centre and Dorling Kindersley would like to thank the following for their valuable help and expertise in the production of this book:

Natalie Leucks and Shaun Mould for their tireless modelling. Joan Butler, Leonard Gonnella, Michael Howard, Rachel Harris, and Fiona Evans (and baby) for modelling on pp.86-87.

Janos Marffy for all artworks and illustrations. Lol Henderson for editorial help, and Maria D'Orsi for design assistance. Liz Wheeler for information on anatomy and medical matters, and Hilary Bird for the index.

Richard Bucknall for photographic assistance, and Frances Prescott for hair styling and make-up.

Dancia International, Gamba, and Splitz for clothing. Nice Irmas for the use of rugs and cushions. Joanne Goff for last-minute alterations.